How the Internet Works

All New Edition

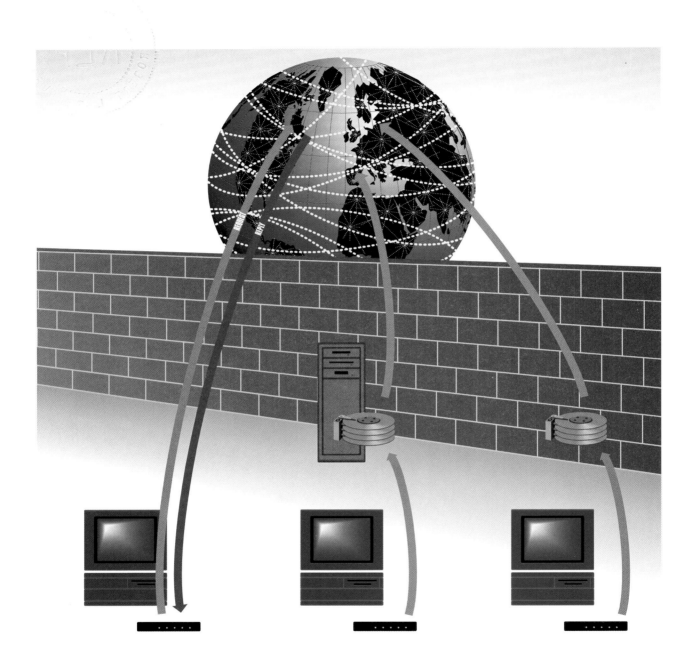

How the Internet Works
All New Edition

Preston Gralla

Illustrated by Sarah Ishida

Ziff-Davis Press
An imprint of Macmillan Computer Publishing USA
Emeryville, California

Acquisitions Editor	Suzanne Anthony
Development Editor	Valerie Haynes Perry
Copy Editor	Margo R. Hill
Technical Reviewer	Mark Butler
Project Coordinator	Madhu Prasher
Proofreader	Barbara Dahl
Cover Illustration	Sarah Ishida
Cover Design	Megan Gandt
Book Design	Carrie English
Technical Illustration	Sarah Ishida and Karl Miyajima
Word Processing	Howard Blechman
Page Layout	M.D. Barrera
Indexer	Carol Burbo

Ziff-Davis Press, ZD Press, and the Ziff-Davis Press logo are trademarks or registered trademarks of, and are licensed to Macmillan Computer Publishing USA by Ziff-Davis Publishing Company, New York, New York.

Ziff-Davis Press imprint books are produced on a Macintosh computer system with the following applications: FrameMaker®, Microsoft® Word, QuarkXPress®, Adobe Illustrator®, Adobe Photoshop®, Adobe Streamline™, MacLink®Plus, Aldus® FreeHand™, Collage Plus™.

Ziff-Davis Press, an imprint of
Macmillan Computer Publishing USA
5903 Christie Avenue
Emeryville, CA 94608

ISBN 1-56276-404-7

Manufactured in the United States of America

10 9 8 7 6 5 4 3 2

This book was produced digitally by Macmillan Computer Publishing and manufactured using 100% computer-to-plate technology (filmless process), by Shepard Poorman Communications Corporation, Indianapolis, Indiana.

THIS book, like the Internet itself, is a collaborative work. My name may be on the cover, but I am far from the only person involved in its creation.

Valerie Haynes Perry, senior development editor at Ziff-Davis Press, deserves much credit for her excellent eye and ear, and her firm yet gentle way of guiding me to use the right approach when explaining technical information.

Without Sarah Ishida and Karl Miyajima, the illustrators, there would be no book, since it is such a visual experience. And many thanks to the entire team at Ziff-Davis Press that produced the book: Margo R. Hill, copy editor, Madhu Prasher, project coordinator, Howard Blechman, word processor, M.D. Barrera, layout artist, and Carol Burbo, indexer.

Thanks also have to go to the many, many people I interviewed for this book. People from Quarterdeck Corporation, Chaco Communications, Progressive Networks, White Pine Software, SurfWatch Software, and VDONet Corp., are only a few of the people who gave their time to help me understand the nitty-gritty of how various Internet technologies work.

I gleaned much information from the many FAQs and similar documents widely available on the Internet. I'd like to thank the anonymous authors of those documents, wherever they are.

Much thanks goes to Mark Butler, the technical editor for the book, who did a superb job of ensuring that I always got the information right.

Finally, big thanks have to go to my wife Lydia, who put up with occasional glassy-eyed looks to simple questions (did you leave your keys in the refrigerator again?) and extreme absent-mindedness because I was figuring out how to explain how a firewall or ISDN or a Web robot works when I should have been concentrating on more immediate matters.

How many times have you wondered—when cruising the World Wide Web and clicking on a link, or transferring a file to your computer via FTP, or reading a newsgroup message, or when hearing about a technology such as firewalls—*How does that work?* How a message sent from your computer can travel through the vastness of cyberspace and end up in the right e-mail box halfway across the world. How you can use search tools to find the exact piece of information you want out of the millions of pieces of information on the whole Internet.

This book will answer all those questions, and many more. It will tell you how every aspect of the Internet works, and will show you how it works in vivid, beautifully detailed illustrations.

The book is designed for everyone interested in the Internet. Its guiding principle is this: No matter how much of a cyberpro you are—or how much of a novice—there's a lot you don't understand about the Internet. Just one small example: A friend of mine, who for several years has made his living with companies involved with the Internet—a complete cyberpro who lives and breathes the Internet—almost whispered to me the other day: "I don't like to admit this, but I don't know what a proxy server is. How *does* it work, anyway?"

If you're like just about everyone else involved in the Internet, you have similar questions. You'll find your answers here.

In Part 1, I explain the underlying basics of the Internet: Who runs it, how TCP/IP works, how to understand Internet addresses and domains, and similar topics.

Part 2 depicts the various ways that you can connect to the Internet. Whether you're interested in learning how ISDN works, how online services connect to the Internet, or a host of similar issues, you'll find out how it all works there.

Part 3 covers every aspect of Internet communications. It shows how e-mail and newsgroups work; how IRC chat works; and how you can use the Internet to make telephone calls anywhere in the world for the price of a local call.

In Part 4 I'll show how the common Internet tools and services work. Here's where you'll find out how the World Wide Web works; how gophers, Telnet, and WAIS work; and what happens when you download a file to your computer using FTP.

Part 5 shows how the cutting-edge and most exciting part of the Internet works: multimedia. Whether you want to know how Virtual Reality video works, how Netcams work, or how the Java programming language works, that's where you'll find it.

Part 6 details the various ways that the Internet is applied, and shows how it's used for business, medicine, and education. And it shows how robots, spiders, and search tools troll the Net for you, gathering information along the way.

Finally, Part 7 covers security concerns. It shows how firewalls work, how viruses can attack your computer, how cryptosystems allow confidential information to be sent across the Internet. And it covers the controversial issue of pornography on the Net—and shows how parental control software can prevent children from seeing objectionable material.

So come along and see how the vast Internet works. Even if you're a cyberpro, you'll find out a lot you never knew.

P A R T

WHAT IS THE INTERNET?

FOR the first time ever, the world is truly at your fingertips. From your computer you can find information about anything you can name or even imagine. You can communicate with people on the other side of the world. You can set up a teleconference, tap into the resources of powerful computers anywhere in the globe, search through the world's best libraries, and visit the world's most amazing museums. You can watch videos and listen to music, and read special multimedia magazines.

You can do all this by tapping into the largest computer network in the world—the Internet.

The Internet isn't a single network; it is a vast, globe-spanning network of networks. No single person, group, or organization runs the Internet. Instead, it's the purest form of electronic democracy. The networks communicate with each other based on certain protocols, such as the Transmission Control Protocol (TCP) and the Internet Protocol (IP). More and more networks and computers are being hooked up to the Internet every day. There are tens of thousands of these networks, ranging from university networks to corporate local area networks to large online services such as America Online and Compu-Serve. Every time you tap into the Internet, your own computer becomes an extension of that network.

In the first section of this book we'll take a close look at what the Internet is. We'll also examine the architectures, protocols, and general concepts that make it all possible.

In Chapter 1 we will examine how the Internet runs. We'll look at who pays for the high-speed data backbones that carry much of the Internet's traffic, and at the organizations that make sure that there are standards for networks to follow so that the Internet can run smoothly. And we'll also look at the various kinds of networks that are connected to the Internet.

Chapter 2 explains how information travels across the Internet. It details how hardware such as routers, repeaters, and bridges sends information among networks. And it shows how smaller networks are grouped into larger regional networks—and how those large regional networks communicate among themselves.

In Chapter 3 we'll look at the Internet's basic protocols for communications, and learn a bit about basic Internet jargon: TCP/IP (short for Transmission Control Protocol and Internet Protocol). The chapter will explain how those protocols work, and how special software such as Winsock allows personal computers to get onto a network originally designed for larger computers.

Chapter 4 takes the mystery out of the Internet's oft-times confusing addressing scheme. You'll learn about Internet domains and addresses, and will even be able to understand how to make sense of them.

Chapter 5 will give you an understanding of the most common types of files you'll come across when browsing the Net. Compressed files, video files, graphics files—you'll learn about just about any kind of file you might encounter.

Whether you're a newbie or cyberpro, this section will teach you the basics of the Internet.

CHAPTER

1

The Wired World of the Internet

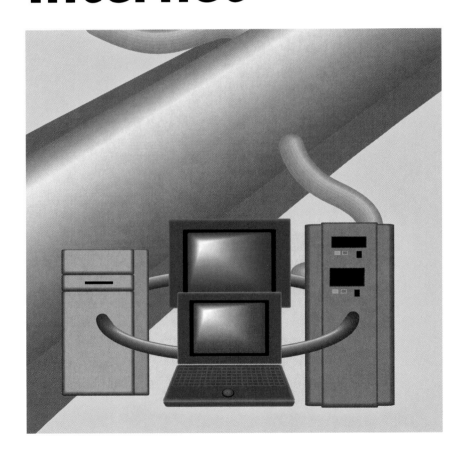

ONE of the most frequently asked questions about the Internet is who runs it? It is inconceivable to most people that no one group or organization runs this vast global network. The truth is that there is no centralized management for the Internet. Instead, it is a collection of thousands of individual networks and organizations, each of which is run and paid for on its own. Each network cooperates with other networks to direct Internet traffic, so that information can pass among them. Together, all these networks and organizations make up the wired world of the Internet. In order for networks and computers to cooperate in this way, though, there needs to be general agreement about things such as Internet procedures and standards for protocols. These procedures and standards are laid out in RFCs (requests for comment) that Internet users and organizations have agreed upon.

A variety of groups guide the Internet's growth by helping to establish standards and educating people on the proper way to use the Internet. Perhaps the most important is the Internet Society, a private, nonprofit group. The Internet Society supports the work of the Internet Activities Board (IAB), which handles much of the Internet's behind-the-scenes and architectural issues. The IAB's Internet Engineering Task Force is responsible for overseeing how the Internet's TCP/IP protocols evolve. The IAB's Internet Research Task force works on network technology. The IAB also has responsibility for assigning network IP addresses through the Internet Assigned Numbers Authority. And it runs the Internet Registry, which runs the Domain Name System, and handles associating domain names with IP addresses.

The World Wide Web Consortium (W3 Consortium) develops standards for the evolution of the fastest growing part of the Internet, the World Wide Web. An industry consortium run by the Laboratory for Computer Science at the Massachusetts Institute of Technology, it collaborates with organizations all over the world, such as CERN, the originators of the Web. It serves as a repository of information about the Web for developers and users; it implements Web standards, and it makes prototypes and uses sample applications to demonstrate new technology.

While these organizations are important as a kind of glue for holding the Internet together, at the heart of the Internet are individual local networks. These networks can be found in private companies, universities, government agencies, and online services. They are funded separately from each other, in a variety of manners, such as fees from users, corporate support, taxes, and grants.

The networks are connected in a variety of ways. For efficiency's sake, local networks join together in consortiums known as regional networks. A variety of leased lines connect regional and local networks. The leased lines that connect networks can be as simple as a single telephone line, or as complex as a fiber optic cable with microwave links and satellite transmissions.

Backbones—very high-capacity lines—carry enormous amounts of Internet traffic. These backbones are paid for by government agencies such as NASA, and by large private corporations. Some backbones are paid for by the National Science Foundation.

How the Internet Runs

1 Since the Internet is a loose organization of networks, no one group runs it and pays for it. Instead, many private organizations, universities, and government agencies pay for and run parts of it. They all work together in a democratic, loosely organized alliance. Private organizations range from small, home-grown networks to commercial online services such as America Online and CompuServe, and private Internet providers who sell access to the Internet.

2 The federal government pays for some high-speed backbones that carry Internet traffic across the country and the world, through agencies such as the National Science Foundation. The extremely high-speed vBNS (very high-speed Backbone Network Services), for example, provides a high-speed infrastructure for the research and education community by linking together supercomputer centers, and will also eventually provide a backbone for commercial applications as well. Often a large corporation or organization such as NASA will also provide backbones to link sites across the country or world.

Regional Network

vBNS Backbone

3 Regional networks provide and maintain Internet access within a geographic area. Regional nets may consist of smaller networks and organizations within the area who have banded together to provide better service.

Supercomputer Center

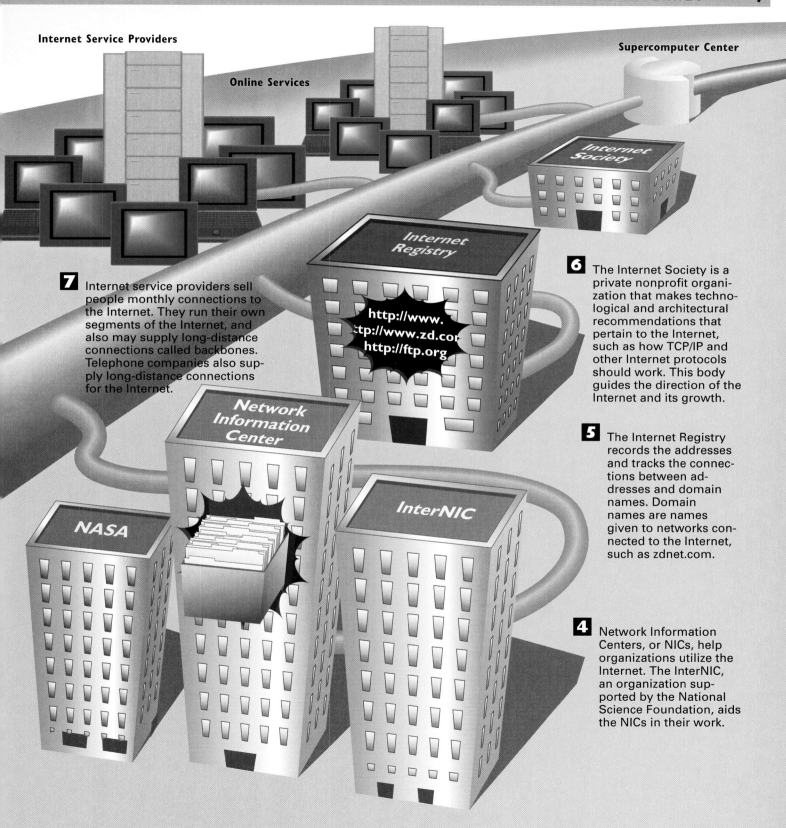

Internet Service Providers

Online Services

Supercomputer Center

Internet
Society

Internet
Registry

http://www.
ttp://www.zd.co
http://ftp.org

Network
Information
Center

NASA

InterNIC

7 Internet service providers sell people monthly connections to the Internet. They run their own segments of the Internet, and also may supply long-distance connections called backbones. Telephone companies also supply long-distance connections for the Internet.

6 The Internet Society is a private nonprofit organization that makes technological and architectural recommendations that pertain to the Internet, such as how TCP/IP and other Internet protocols should work. This body guides the direction of the Internet and its growth.

5 The Internet Registry records the addresses and tracks the connections between addresses and domain names. Domain names are names given to networks connected to the Internet, such as zdnet.com.

4 Network Information Centers, or NICs, help organizations utilize the Internet. The InterNIC, an organization supported by the National Science Foundation, aids the NICs in their work.

C H A P T E R
2

How Information Travels across the Internet

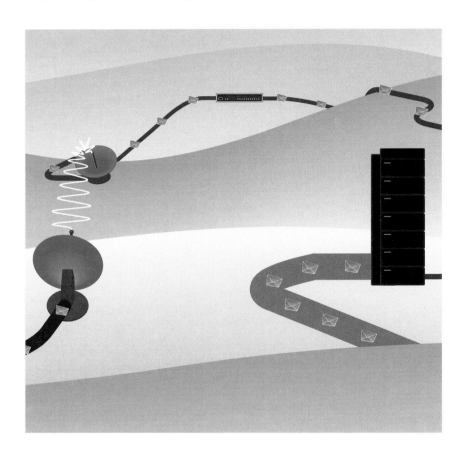

YOU may take it for granted that when you send a piece of information across the Internet it will always reach its intended destination. But the process of sending that information is remarkably complex.

When you send information across the Internet, it is first broken up into packets by the Transmission Control Protocol (TCP). Those packets are sent from your computer to your local network, Internet service provider, or online service. From there, they are sent through many levels of networks, computers, and communications lines before they reach their final destination—a destination that may be across town or around the world. A variety of pieces of hardware processes those packets and routes them to their proper destinations. This hardware is designed to transmit data between networks, and makes up much of the glue that holds the Internet together. Five of the most important pieces are hubs, bridges, gateways, repeaters, and routers.

Hubs are important because they link groups of computers to one another, and let computers communicate with one another. *Bridges* link local area networks (LANs) with one another. They let data destined for another LAN to be sent there, while at the same time keeping local data inside its own network. *Gateways* are similar to bridges, but they also translate data from one kind of network to another.

When data travels across the Internet, it often crosses great distances, which can be a problem because the signal sending it can weaken over the distance. To solve the problem, *repeaters* amplify the data at intervals so that the signal doesn't weaken.

Routers play a key role in managing Internet traffic. Their job is to make sure that the packets always arrive at the proper destination. If data is being transferred among computers that are on the same local area network, routers often aren't needed, because the network itself can handle its internal traffic. But when the data is sent between two different networks, routers come into play. Routers examine packets to find out what their destination is. Taking into account how busy the Internet is, they send the packets to another router, one which is closer to the packet's final destination.

So-called mid-level networks hook LANs together using high-speed telephone lines, Ethernet, and microwave links. A mid-level network in a geographic area is called a regional network, while an organization with many networked sites linked together is another kind of mid-level network, often called a WAN (wide area network).

When a packet travels from a computer on a LAN in a mid-level network to a computer somewhere else on the mid-level network, a router (or a series of routers) sends the packets to their proper destination. If, however, the destination lies outside the mid-level network, the packets are sent to a NAP (Network Access Point), where it is sent across the country or the world on a backbone. High-speed backbones such as the vBNS (very high speed Backbone Network Service) can transmit enormous amounts of data—155 megabits (millions of bits) per second.

Linking Networks to the Internet

1 The Internet comprises networks that are attached to one another via pathways that facilitate the exchange of information, data, and files. Being connected to the Internet means having access to these pathways. Using these pathways, your computer can send packets of data over these pathways to any other computer connected to the Internet.

2 You get onto the Internet either through a local area network at your place of business, or by dialing into a large computer connected to the Internet via an online service or a dial-in Internet provider. Many different kinds of networks can be connected to the Internet, such as ethernet networks, token-ring networks, and others. In token-ring networks, data is passed in "tokens" from computer to computer in a ring or star configuration. In Ethernet networks, the data instead goes from a server to a computer on the network.

3 Routers, which connect networks, perform most of the work of directing traffic on the Internet. Routers examine the packets of data that travel across the Internet to see where the data is headed. Based on the data's destination, it routes it the most efficient way—generally to another router, which in turn sends it to the next router, and so on.

4 Networks are connected in many different ways. There are dedicated telephone lines that can transmit data at 56 kilobits per second. There are an increasing number of T1 leased telephone lines that carry data between networks. A T1 link can carry 1.544 megabits of data per second. Higher-speed T3 links, which can carry data at 44.746 megabits per second, are being used as well.

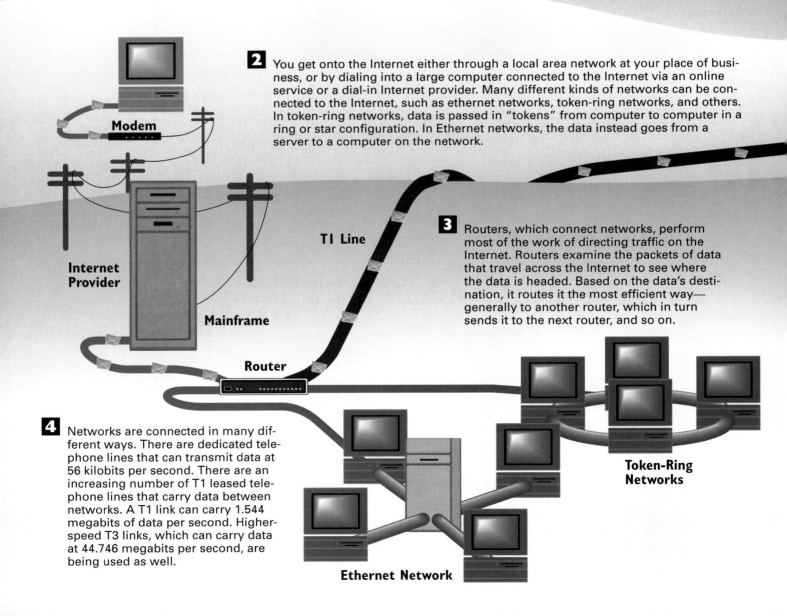

Modem

Internet Provider

Mainframe

T1 Line

Router

Token-Ring Networks

Ethernet Network

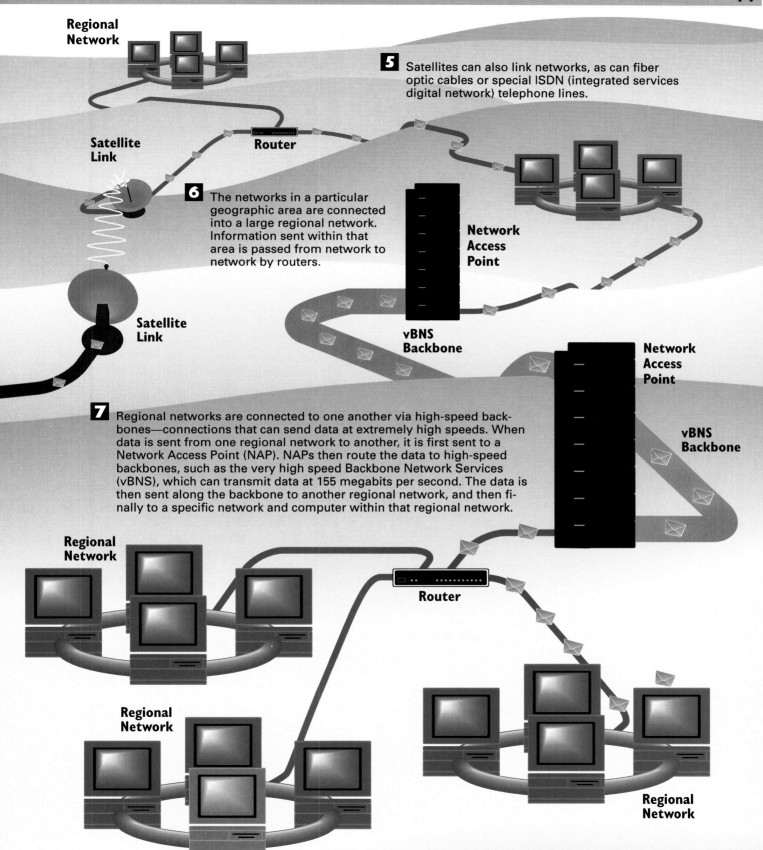

Regional Network

5 Satellites can also link networks, as can fiber optic cables or special ISDN (integrated services digital network) telephone lines.

Satellite Link

Router

6 The networks in a particular geographic area are connected into a large regional network. Information sent within that area is passed from network to network by routers.

Network Access Point

vBNS Backbone

Satellite Link

Network Access Point

vBNS Backbone

7 Regional networks are connected to one another via high-speed backbones—connections that can send data at extremely high speeds. When data is sent from one regional network to another, it is first sent to a Network Access Point (NAP). NAPs then route the data to high-speed backbones, such as the very high speed Backbone Network Services (vBNS), which can transmit data at 155 megabits per second. The data is then sent along the backbone to another regional network, and then finally to a specific network and computer within that regional network.

Regional Network

Regional Network

Router

Regional Network

C H A P T E R

3

How TCP/IP, Winsock, and MacTCP Work

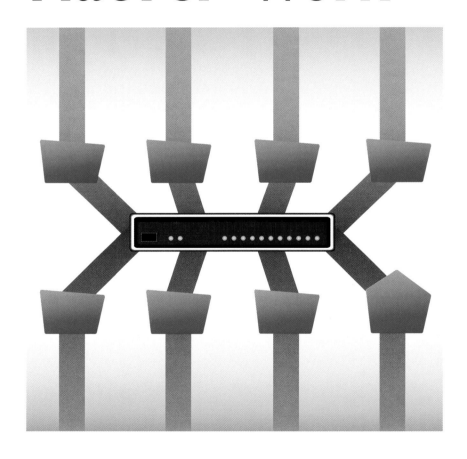

THE ability of computers and networks all over the world to share information and messages on the Internet is made possible by a seemingly simple set of ideas: Break up every piece of information and message into pieces called packets, deliver those packets to the proper destinations, and then reassemble the packets into their original form after they've been delivered, so that they can be viewed and used by the receiver. That's what the two most important communications protocols on the Internet do—the Transmission Control Protocol (TCP) and the Internet Protocol (IP). They are frequently referred to as TCP/IP. TCP breaks down and reassembles the packets, while IP is responsible for making sure that the packets are sent to the right destination.

TCP/IP is used because the Internet is what is known as a *packet-switched* network. In a packet-switched network, there is no single, unbroken connection between sender and receiver. Instead, when information is sent, it is broken into small packets, sent over many different routes at the same time, and then reassembled at the receiving end. By contrast, the telephone system is a *circuit-switched* network. In a circuit-switched network, once a connection is made (as with a telephone call, for example), that part of the network is dedicated only to that single connection.

In order for personal computers to take full advantage of the Internet, they need to use special software that understands and interprets the Internet's TCP/IP protocols. This software is referred to as a *socket* or a *TCP/IP stack*. For PCs, the required software is called Winsock. There are many different versions of Winsock available for PCs. For Macintoshes, the software is called MacTCP. In both cases, this software serves as an intermediary between the Internet and the personal computer. Personal computers can take advantage of some parts of the Internet without having to use Winsock or MacTCP—but only the simplest, most rudimentary parts. For full access to the Internet, TCP/IP stacks are necessary.

A computer can be connected to a local area network with a network card. In order to communicate with the network, the network card requires a *hardware driver*—software that mediates between the network and the network card. If a computer is not physically connected to a local area network with a network card, it can instead connect to the Internet by dialing in and using a modem. It will still need a TCP/IP stack in order for the computer to use the TCP/IP protocols. It won't require a network card, however, and so won't need a hardware driver. Instead, it needs to use one of two software protocols: either SLIP (Serial Line Internet Protocol) or PPP (Point-to-Point Protocol). These protocols are designed for computers connected to the Internet over a serial connection via a modem. In general, the newer PPP protocol provides a more error-free connection than does the older SLIP. Computers can also dial into the Internet without using TCP/IP stacks or SLIP or PPP protocols, but then they won't be able to tap into the full power of the Internet.

How TCP/IP Works

1 The Internet is what is known as a *packet-switched* network. This means that when you send information across the Internet, the data is broken into small packets. Each packet is sent independently of one another through a series of switches called routers. Once all the packets arrive at the receiving end, they are recombined into their original, unified form. Two protocols do the work of breaking the data into packets, routing it across the Internet, and then recombining them on the other end: The Internet Protocol (IP), which handles the routing of the data; and the Transmission Control Protocol (TCP), which handles breaking the data into packets and recombining the packets on the receiving end.

2 For a number of reasons, including hardware limitations, data sent across the Internet must be broken up into packets of less than about 1,500 characters each. TCP does the job of taking data and breaking it up into packets. Each packet is given a header which contains a variety of information, such as in what order the packets should be assembled with other related packets. As TCP creates each packet, it also calculates and adds to the header a *checksum*, which is a number that TCP uses on the receiving end to determine whether any errors have been introduced into the packet during transmission. The checksum is based on the precise amount of data in the packet.

Header

| 23,578 | 12,333 | 14,132 | 17,136 |

3 Each packet is put into separate IP "envelopes." These envelopes contain addressing information that tells the Internet where to send the data. All of the envelopes for a given piece of data have the same addressing information so that they can all be sent to the same location to be reassembled. IP "envelopes" contain headers which include information such as the sender address, the destination address, the amount of time the packet should be kept before discarding it, and other information.

IP Envelopes

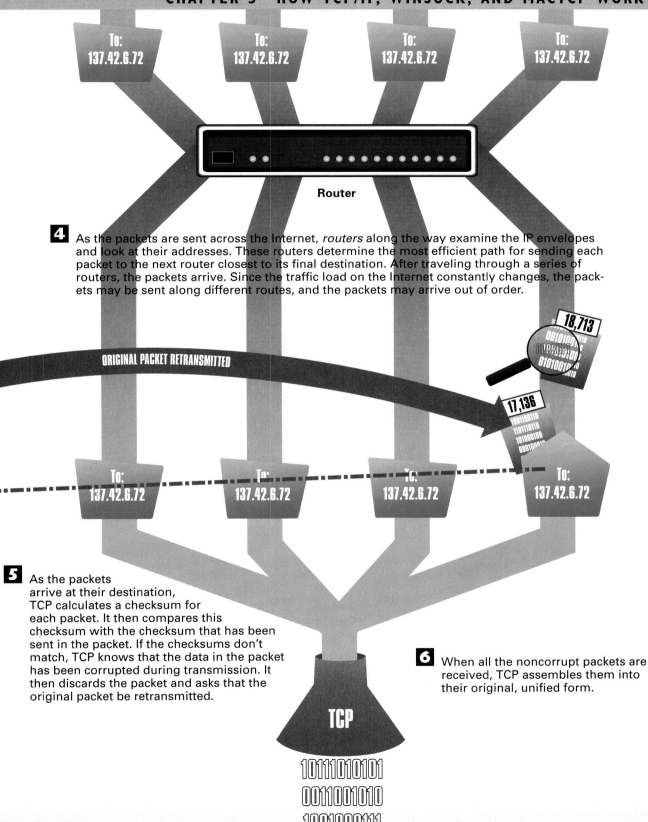

To:
137.42.6.72

To:
137.42.6.72

To:
137.42.6.72

To:
137.42.6.72

Router

4 As the packets are sent across the Internet, *routers* along the way examine the IP envelopes and look at their addresses. These routers determine the most efficient path for sending each packet to the next router closest to its final destination. After traveling through a series of routers, the packets arrive. Since the traffic load on the Internet constantly changes, the packets may be sent along different routes, and the packets may arrive out of order.

18,713

ORIGINAL PACKET RETRANSMITTED

17,136

To:
137.42.6.72

To:
137.42.6.72

To:
137.42.6.72

To:
137.42.6.72

5 As the packets arrive at their destination, TCP calculates a checksum for each packet. It then compares this checksum with the checksum that has been sent in the packet. If the checksums don't match, TCP knows that the data in the packet has been corrupted during transmission. It then discards the packet and asks that the original packet be retransmitted.

6 When all the noncorrupt packets are received, TCP assembles them into their original, unified form.

TCP

1011010101
0011001010
1001000111
1011000101

CHAPTER

4

Understanding Internet Addresses and Domains

To do just about anything on the Internet—and especially to send electronic mail—you'll need to understand Internet addresses. The Internet Protocol (IP) uses Internet address information to deliver mail and other information from computer to computer. Every IP address on the Internet is actually a series of four numbers separated by periods (called *dots*), such as 163.52.128.72. It would be difficult, if not impossible, for you to remember numeric addresses when you wanted to get in touch with someone. Also, sometimes numeric IP addresses change, and it would be impossible for people to keep track not only of the original numeric addresses, but also to know every time those numeric addresses change. To solve these problems, an easier way has been developed to keep track of addresses: *The Domain Name System* (DNS).

The Domain Name System establishes a hierarchy of *domains*—groups of computers on the Internet. And it gives each computer on the Internet a *domain name* (also known as an Internet address) using easily recognizable letters and words instead of numbers. The domains at the top level of the hierarchy maintain lists and addresses of the domains just beneath them. Those domains just beneath them have similar responsibilities for the domains just beneath *them* and so on, and in this way every computer on the Internet gets a domain name. The DNS also helps Internet computers to send mail to the proper destination by converting the textual Internet address into its IP numeric equivalent.

As an example of how the DNS works, here's NASA's SPACElink Internet address: spacelink.msfc.nasa.gov. The top domain is *gov*, which stands for government. The domain just below that is *nasa*, which is the NASA domain. Then below that, *msfc* (Marshall Space Flight Center) is one of NASA's many computer networks. *Spacelink* identifies the NASA computer that runs the SPACElink program. SPACElink's numeric IP address has changed through the years, but its domain name has stayed the same. The DNS system keeps track of changes like this, so that even when an IP address changes, if the domain name is used, mail will always be delivered to the proper place. Computers called *name servers* are responsible for keeping track of such changes, and translating between IP addresses and domain addresses.

Now that we've looked at domain names, let's examine e-mail addresses. E-mail addresses use the @ (at) sign to identify a person's address at a specific computer on the Internet. The spacelink.msfc.nasa.gov computer, for example, may have many people who use it to maintain e-mail boxes. Every person with an e-mail box on that computer is identified by their name, then the @ sign, and finally the location of the computer. The system administrator of the computer establishes the e-mail name for each user of the computer. To send e-mail to Fred Pfizer with an e-mail box on that system, you'd send e-mail to fpfizer@spacelink.msfc.nasa.gov, or fred_pfizer@spacelink.msfc.nasa.gov, depending on the name that the system administrator established. When you send e-mail to him, it will be stored on the spacelink.msfc.nasa.gov computer and he can get it when he logs on.

Understanding Internet Addresses and Domains

1 The Internet Protocol (IP) delivers mail based on the specific address of the e-mail. The address is expressed as four numbers, separated by periods (called *dots*), such as 163.52.128.72. However, since it would be difficult to remember such complex addresses, you can instead use Internet addresses made up of words and letters. Computers called *name servers* translate the word address into a numerical address, so e-mail can be sent to the proper location.

2 An Internet address is made up of two major parts separated by an @ (pronounced *at*) sign. The address can tell you a good deal of information about the person whose address it is. The first part of the address—to the left of the @ sign—is the *user name* which usually refers to the person who holds the Internet account, and is often that person's login name. The second part of the address, to the right of the @ sign, contains the *host name*, followed by the *domain name*, which together identifies the specific computer where the person has an Internet mail account.

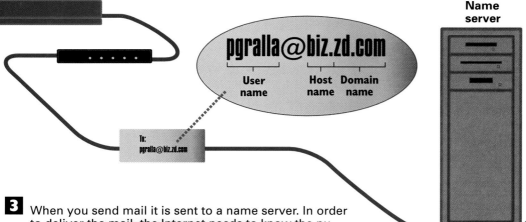

Name server

pgralla@biz.zd.com

User name   Host name   Domain name

To:
pgralla@biz.zd.com

3 When you send mail it is sent to a name server. In order to deliver the mail, the Internet needs to know the numeric IP address. Name servers look up the word address, and substitute the numeric IP address for it so that the mail can be delivered properly.

4 The Domain Name System is a way of dividing the Internet into understandable groups, or domains. The far rightmost portion of the domain section of the address identifies the largest domain and kind of organization where the person's address is.

5 To the left of the largest domain is information that gives specific information about the organization, and so tells routers to which network the mail should be sent. It can be a single domain name, such as zd (for Ziff-Davis). Or it can be a group of domains and subdomains, such as mfsc.nasa.

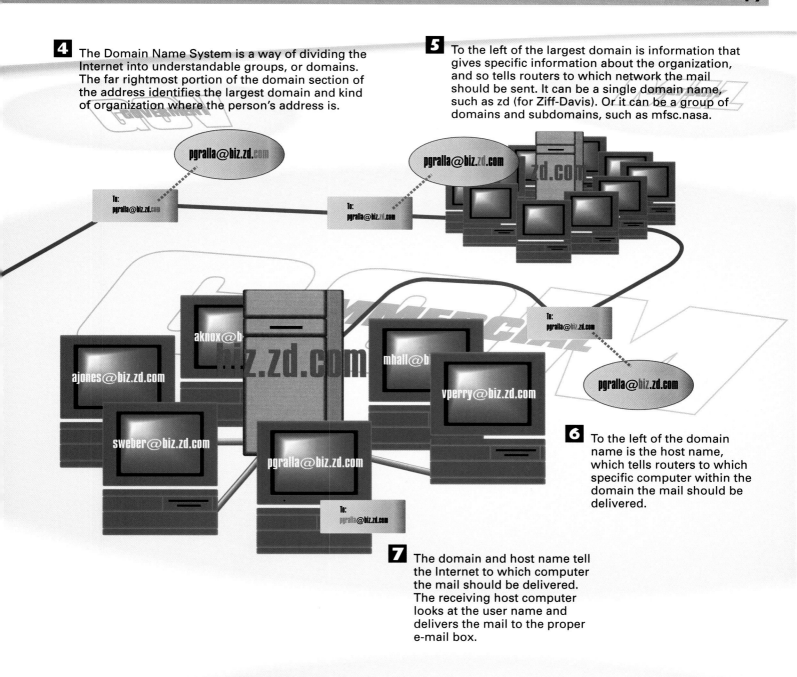

6 To the left of the domain name is the host name, which tells routers to which specific computer within the domain the mail should be delivered.

7 The domain and host name tell the Internet to which computer the mail should be delivered. The receiving host computer looks at the user name and delivers the mail to the proper e-mail box.

NOTE Common domains in the United States are *com* for commercial; *edu* for education; *gov* for government; *mil* for military; *net* for network (companies and groups concerned with the organization of the Internet); and *org* for organization. Outside the United States, only two letters are used to identify the domains, such as *au* for Australia; *ca* for Canada; *uk* for United Kingdom; and *fr* for France.

5

Internet File Types

THERE are millions of files on the Internet that show you pictures, let you hear music and sounds, allow you to watch videos, and let you read articles and run software on your computer. Some of these files can be used on any computer, regardless of whether it is a Macintosh or an IBM-compatible PC. Graphics files, sound files, and video files, for example, can be played on many different kinds of computers, as long as those computers have the special software (often called *players*) required to view, run, or listen to them. Some files require special hardware in order to work. Other files, such as software programs that you download, for example, can only be run on a specific model of computer.

In general, on the Internet you'll find three kinds of files: ASCII (American Standard Code for Information Interchange); EBCDIC (Extended Binary Coded Decimal Interchange Code); and binary. ASCII and EBCDIC are ways of organizing data into something that is understandable to us. ASCII codes are computer codes that stand for the characters on your screen, such as the uppercase letter A or a dollar sign ($). ASCII text files contain nothing but simple character data. They lack the sophisticated formatting commands that word processing or desktop publishing programs can apply to a document. EBCDIC is like ASCII but you won't normally find EBCDIC files since they're primarily used by mainframe computers. Binary files are files that contain special coded data and can only be run or read by specific computers and software.

In contrast to plain ASCII text files there are files that contain sophisticated formatting and graphical information in them. Files that adhere to the *PostScript page description language* are of this type. These files are in fact ASCII files, but they contain information about how to format and print the file. There are other kinds of files that contain formatting and graphical information, such as those in the Adobe Acrobat format, but many of them are binary files instead of ASCII files. In order to view or print either of these types of file, you'll need special software readers—and in the case of PostScript files, you'll generally need a special PostScript printer that knows how to print files in that language. Files of this type can be viewed in two ways: either when you're online and connected to the Internet, or when you're offline and not connected. To view the files when online, you'll use special plug-in modules or helper applications for your Web browser. To view the files when offline, you'll need software readers.

Sound, visual image, animation, and video files are also common on the Internet. These files are all binary files, which are made up of bits that are represented by 0's and 1's. Files of this type are often large, and require special software readers and players and sometimes hardware in order to play and read them. Some of these files can only be played or viewed on a specific type of computer, while others can be played or viewed on many types of computers if you have the right software. Some of the files, such as streaming audio files and streaming video files, can be viewed while you're online connected to the Internet, while other types need to be viewed when you're offline, with special readers or players.

File Types on the Internet

1 There are many different types of files on the Internet. Each file has information contained in its header. The header is simply the first line of a file or a specific number of bytes at the beginning of a file. Software that can read or view the files looks into the header of a file to distinguish what kind of file it is, and then processes the file accordingly.

2 You'll find graphics files in many formats, including GIF, JPEG, PCX, and TIF. GIF and JPEG are two of the most common graphics formats. They allow the exchange of image files between different kinds of computers, and can be downloaded to your computer quickly. A GIF reader or JPEG reader reads binary GIF and JPEG files and displays them on your computer. There are many different GIF and JPEG readers for many different kinds of computers. Graphics programs will typically read both types of files. A GIF file contains the binary data that when viewed with the proper reader will display a picture of the space shuttle. Your computer's video card takes the information from the reader and displays it on your computer's monitor.

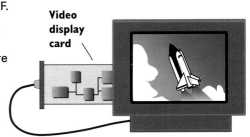

Video display card

Software engine

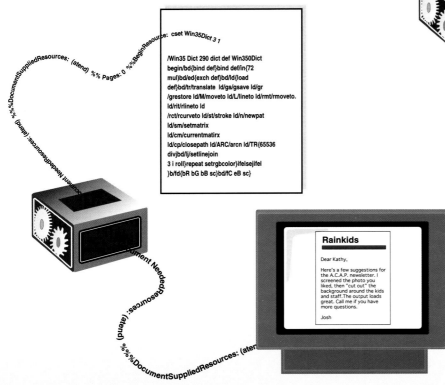

```
cset Win35Dict 3 1

/Win35 Dict 290 dict def Win350Dict
begin/bd{bind def}bind def/in{72
mul}bd/ed{exch def}bd/ld{load
def}bd/tr/translate ld/gs/gsave ld/gr
/grestore ld/M/moveto ld/L/lineto ld/rmt/rmoveto.
ld/rit/rlineto ld
/rct/rcurveto ld/st/stroke ld/n/newpat
ld/sm/setmatrix
ld/cm/currentmatirx
ld/cp/closepath ld/ARC/arcn ld/TR{65536
div}bd/lj/setlinejoin
3 i roll}repeat setrgbcolor}ifelsejifel
}b/fd{bR bG bB sc}bd/fC eB sc}
```

Rainkids

Dear Kathy,

Here's a few suggestions for the A.C.A.P. newsletter. I screened the photo you liked, then "cut out" the background around the kids and staff. The output loads great. Call me if you have more questions.

Josh

3 Several different file types, such as PostScript (which ends in a .PS extension) and Adobe Acrobat (which ends in a .PDF extension), contain complex information about documents, including placement of pictures, size and type of fonts, and the complex shapes and formatting information that is needed in order to view the page. You'll need special software to open up PostScript, Acrobat, and similar files. For PostScript, you'll need a PostScript reader. For Acrobat, you'll need an Acrobat reader. These readers will allow you to see the fully formatted page on your screen over the Internet, and print them if you wish.

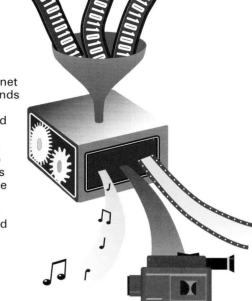

4 You'll find many different kinds of binary multimedia files on the Internet that let you listen to or play sounds, music, and videos. Windows sounds files (which end in a .WAV extension) and Macintosh sound files are common types of sound files that you download to your computer and play with a sound player. Other sound files, such as those created by Real Audio software, allow you to listen to the sounds while the file is downloading—called streaming audio. You'll need special software to run streaming audio. Common video and animation files are Windows animations files (which end in an .AVI extension) Macintosh QuickTime videos and MPEG files (which end in an .MPG extension). They all require special software players in order to view them. Other animation files allow you to watch the video while the file is downloading—called streaming video.

PROGRAM.ZIP

Uncompression engine

Program.exe

5 There are many *executable programs* you'll find on the Internet—software that you can download to your computer and use, just like any other kind of software. Since this software can be large and take a long time to download, it is often compressed to make it download faster. Once it's on your computer, you uncompress it with special decompression software, and run it like any other program. Frequently, PC software has been compressed with PKZIP, and has a .ZIP extension, while Macintosh software can be compressed with a variety of compression software. In general, PC files can only be used with PCs, while Macintosh files can only be used with Macintoshes.

6 You'll find many *text files* on the Internet—ASCII files that you can read with a text editor or word processor. These can be articles, FAQs (frequently asked questions and their answers), or any other kind of informational files.

Dear Kathy,

Here's a few suggestions for the A.C.A.P. newsletter. I screened the photo you liked, then "cut out" the background around the kids and staff. The output loads great. Call me if you have more questions.

Josh

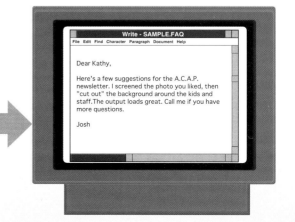

Write - SAMPLE.FAQ
File Edit Find Character Paragraph Document Help

Dear Kathy,

Here's a few suggestions for the A.C.A.P. newsletter. I screened the photo you liked, then "cut out" the background around the kids and staff. The output loads great. Call me if you have more questions.

Josh

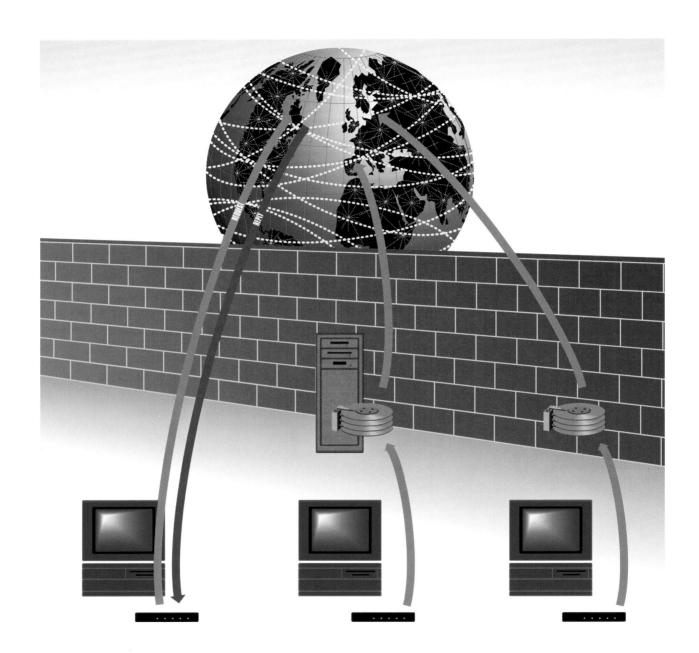

P A R T

CONNECTING TO THE INTERNET

So now you know what the Internet is, and what it has to offer. But how do you actually connect to it?

There are many ways to connect to the Internet. You can have a direct connection at your place of work or university. You can be connected via telephone lines at home. Your computer can be merely a "dumb terminal" that can gain access to only a few Internet resources, or your computer can be a full Internet computer, with access to everything the Internet has to offer. In this part of the book we'll look at the myriad ways that people and computers gain access to the Internet.

There's one general rule about Internet connections: The faster the better. Especially since there are many pictures, sounds, and videos on the Internet, people want the fastest connection possible. Today, the two most common ways you can connect to the Internet are through a corporate or university local area network, or over telephone lines. Direct connections over local area networks are generally faster than telephone line connections.

In this section we'll look at all the ways that computers can connect to the Internet. Chapter 6 gives an overview of the different kinds of Internet connections that are possible. Not only will we examine many different kinds of network connections and phone line connections, but we'll also look at newer, high-speed connections that are becoming available; cable modems are one example of this.

Online services such as CompuServe, America Online, and Microsoft Network at one time competed directly with the Internet. But now those online services, instead of competing, have joined the Internet club. An online service can be one of the simplest ways to get an Internet connection. When you connect to an online service, you also get a full connection to the Internet. Chapter 7 examines how online services make that Internet connection.

Someday we all expect to have extremely high-speed connections to the Internet, possibly via fiber optic cabling into our homes. However, this will cost billions of dollars, and that ability appears to be many years away. A quicker solution to reasonably priced high-speed connections is *ISDN*, short for Integrated Services Digital Network. ISDN lets us connect at high speeds to the Internet via normal, existing telephone lines. Not every area in the country has ISDN yet. In some areas, it can be an expensive option, while in others it is reasonably priced. It requires a special modem as well. But it is an increasingly popular way to get at the Internet at very high speeds—much faster than even the highest speed modems. Chapter 8 explains how ISDN works.

CHAPTER

6

Connecting Your Computer

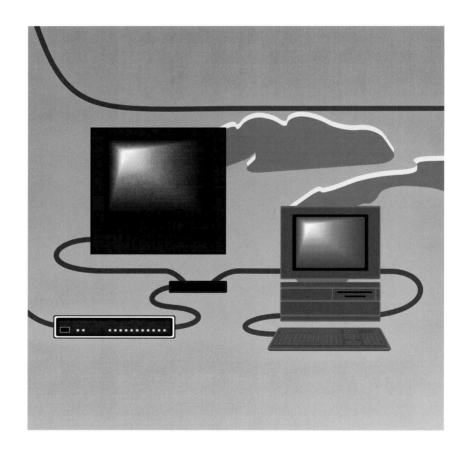

THERE are many different ways that your computer can connect to the Internet, ranging from dial-in connections to LAN connections to connections over cable TV wires. If you are connected to a LAN or campus network at your business or school, you may already be connected to the Internet. If the network is connected to the Internet via a router or bridge, that means your computer is also connected. Often, this offers a higher-speed access than when you dial in to the Internet directly. If you're not connected to the Internet via a network, there are a variety of options for accessing the Internet—and many more appear every day. Most use modems and the general telephone system.

One option is to find a network or Internet provider that lets you dial into it with *terminal emulation software*. When you do this, your computer functions like a "dumb terminal," and the Internet software doesn't actually run on your computer. Instead, you run it on the computer you've connected to, and your screen merely shows what's happening on the computer you've dialed into. If you connect this way, the Internet services you can access are severely limited—for example, you generally won't be able to see graphics while you browse the most popular part of the Internet—the World Wide Web.

If you want to tap the full power of the Internet over telephone lines, you'll want a full Internet connection, such as you get with SLIP (*Serial Line Internet Protocol*) and PPP (*Point-to-Point Protocol*) connections. When you dial into the Internet with these protocols, your computer becomes a part of the Internet, and you can use all the processing power of your computer. You'll be able to browse the World Wide Web. PPP is newer and more stable than SLIP and can retransmit packets if they get garbled, a not-uncommon situation when sending information over telephone lines.

If you're looking for even higher-speed connections to the Internet, you have two additional choices. ISDN (Integrated Services Digital Network) lines are special digital telephone lines that allow you to dial into the Internet at very high speeds. Typically, these speeds range from 64 kbps to 128 kbps. To use one of these lines, you'll need a special ISDN modem and an Internet provider that offers ISDN access.

Another option is a cable modem, which allows you to use your coaxial television cable to access the Internet. You'll need a special cable modem, and your local cable company will have to have this capability in order for you to access the Internet over cable TV wires. Speeds can be up to 100 times faster than regular modem speeds.

There are many different kinds of connections you can hook up to the Internet with. Start at your local college or library when looking for your own connection. Contact an *Internet Service Provider* (a commercial company that provides access to the Internet for a fee.) There are many national and local service providers, so shop around. And the major online services now include Internet access, so you can easily connect to the Net through them.

Connecting Your Computer to the Internet

There are many different ways to connect to the Internet, ranging from going through a local area network, to several kinds of dial-in connections, to cable modems and special high-speed ISDN lines. Internet service providers can give you telephone SLIP or PPP connections. And all the major online services now offer you an Internet connection as part of their subscription service.

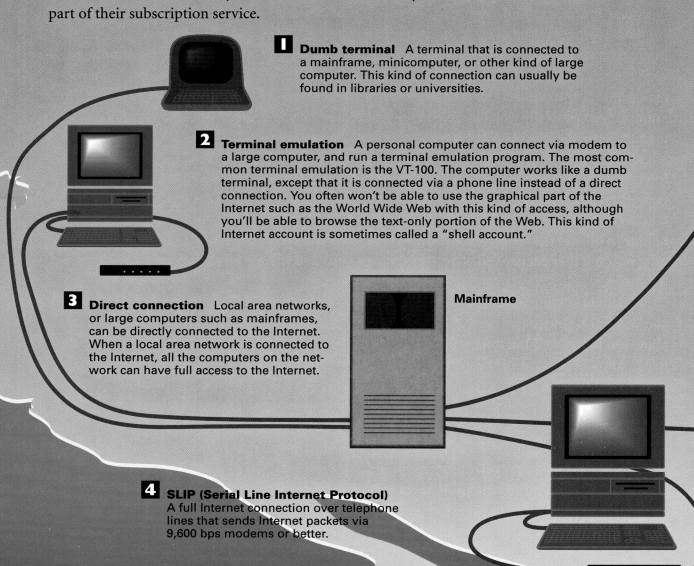

1 Dumb terminal A terminal that is connected to a mainframe, minicomputer, or other kind of large computer. This kind of connection can usually be found in libraries or universities.

2 Terminal emulation A personal computer can connect via modem to a large computer, and run a terminal emulation program. The most common terminal emulation is the VT-100. The computer works like a dumb terminal, except that it is connected via a phone line instead of a direct connection. You often won't be able to use the graphical part of the Internet such as the World Wide Web with this kind of access, although you'll be able to browse the text-only portion of the Web. This kind of Internet account is sometimes called a "shell account."

3 Direct connection Local area networks, or large computers such as mainframes, can be directly connected to the Internet. When a local area network is connected to the Internet, all the computers on the network can have full access to the Internet.

Mainframe

4 SLIP (Serial Line Internet Protocol) A full Internet connection over telephone lines that sends Internet packets via 9,600 bps modems or better.

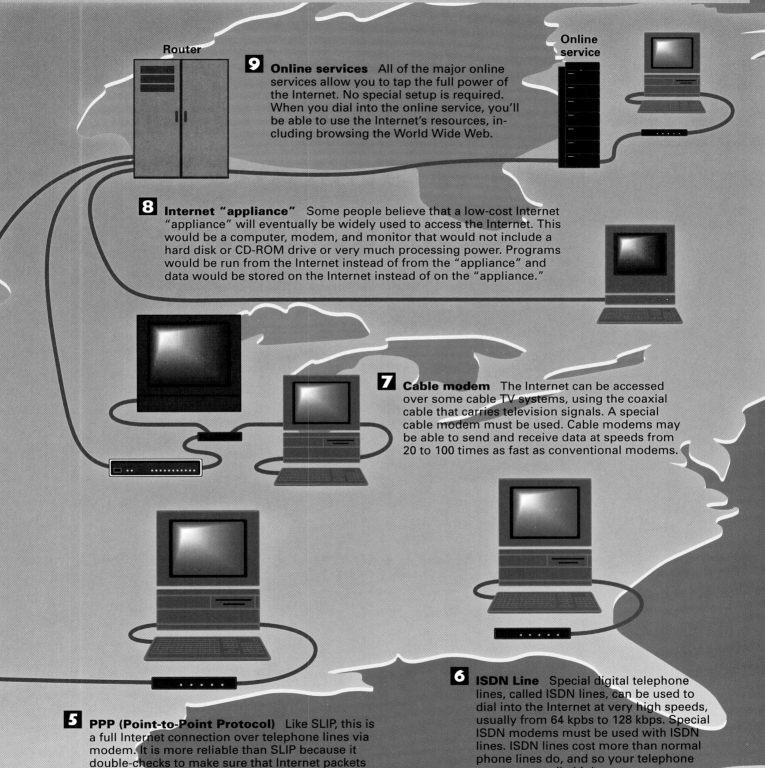

Router

Online service

9 **Online services** All of the major online services allow you to tap the full power of the Internet. No special setup is required. When you dial into the online service, you'll be able to use the Internet's resources, including browsing the World Wide Web.

8 **Internet "appliance"** Some people believe that a low-cost Internet "appliance" will eventually be widely used to access the Internet. This would be a computer, modem, and monitor that would not include a hard disk or CD-ROM drive or very much processing power. Programs would be run from the Internet instead of from the "appliance" and data would be stored on the Internet instead of on the "appliance."

7 **Cable modem** The Internet can be accessed over some cable TV systems, using the coaxial cable that carries television signals. A special cable modem must be used. Cable modems may be able to send and receive data at speeds from 20 to 100 times as fast as conventional modems.

5 **PPP (Point-to-Point Protocol)** Like SLIP, this is a full Internet connection over telephone lines via modem. It is more reliable than SLIP because it double-checks to make sure that Internet packets arrive intact. It resends any damaged packets.

6 **ISDN Line** Special digital telephone lines, called ISDN lines, can be used to dial into the Internet at very high speeds, usually from 64 kpbs to 128 kbps. Special ISDN modems must be used with ISDN lines. ISDN lines cost more than normal phone lines do, and so your telephone rates are usually higher.

CHAPTER

7

Connecting to the Internet from Online Services

THERE are many ways to get access to the Internet – and one of the best is to use an online service such as CompuServe, America Online, Prodigy, or Microsoft Network. These online services have long provided their own unique content, special areas, and services available only to their subscribers. They use proprietary software and interfaces to let subscribers use their resources. Unlike most of the Internet, the content, areas, and services the online companies provide are not free. In order to get them, you have to pay a monthly subscription fee to the online service, and often pay for the number of hours you use the service each month.

The services let you access the Internet in a number of ways. To make it easier to use the Internet's resources, they use their own proprietary software as a way to get at Internet services such as Telnet, gopher, and UseNet newsgroups. When you use the Internet like this, you issue a command using the online service's software. That command is then sent out over a gateway to the Internet. The information you've asked for is retrieved, sent back over the gateway to your online service, and is displayed for you using the online service's proprietary software.

Most online services also allow you to get at the Internet another way. They let you use your own client software to get at Internet resources such as Telnet, gopher, and UseNet newsgroups. To do this, you essentially bypass the online service's proprietary interface. You use the online service as you would a dial-in Internet provider. You dial into the online service to establish a TCP/IP connection. Then you launch the Telnet, gopher, UseNet, or other client software on your computer, and you get at the Internet's resources using the TCP/IP connection that you've established by dialing in.

Online services also let you browse the Web. Some let you use their own proprietary Web browsers. Others have their own proprietary Web browsers, but also allow you to browse the Web using any Web browser of your choice. To use your own Web browser, you first dial into the service to establish a TCP/IP connection. Then you launch your own Web browser, and you can browse the Web just as you would using any other dial-in Internet provider.

How Online Services Connect to the Internet

1 A very convenient way to use Internet resources is to do so through an online service such as CompuServe, America Online, or Microsoft Network. These services provide access to the Internet in several ways. They have their own software to make it easy to access Internet resources such as Telnet, gopher, and FTP. They also allow you to browse the World Wide Web, either by using their own proprietary Web browser, or by using any other Web browser. And some also allow you to use your own Telnet, FTP, gopher or other software if you'd prefer to use your own software instead of theirs. Some also let you use special software to get access to Internet resources such as Internet Relay Chat (IRC) that the online service itself might not provide.

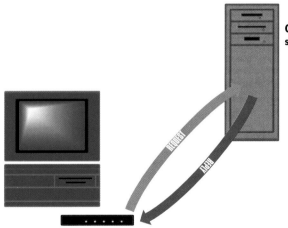

Online service

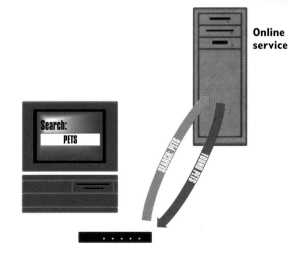

Online service

2 Each online service has a great deal of resources, content, and special areas that are not available to anyone except people who subscribe to that particular service. These areas use the online service's own proprietary software and interface, and do not work like the Internet. You dial directly into the online service to get at these resources.

3 When you use the resources of an online service, you don't go outside the service to the Internet—instead you stay behind a firewall. A *firewall* is a security system of accepting or blocking packets as they are transmitted across a network. Individual online services establish firewalls that only let subscribers into the service.

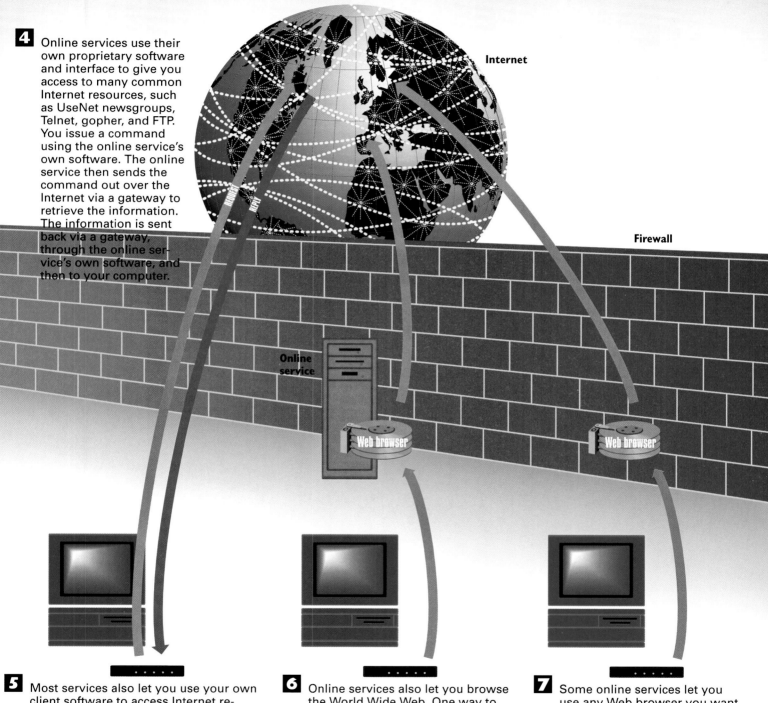

4 Online services use their own proprietary software and interface to give you access to many common Internet resources, such as UseNet newsgroups, Telnet, gopher, and FTP. You issue a command using the online service's own software. The online service then sends the command out over the Internet via a gateway to retrieve the information. The information is sent back via a gateway, through the online service's own software, and then to your computer.

Internet

Firewall

Online service

Web browser

Web browser

5 Most services also let you use your own client software to access Internet resources such as Telnet, gopher, and FTP, and to access Internet resources such as Internet Relay Chat that the services do not have proprietary software for. In order to do this, you dial into the online service and establish a TCP/IP connection. You can then get directly onto the Internet using your own client software.

6 Online services also let you browse the World Wide Web. One way to browse the Web is to use the online service's own proprietary Web browser. Typically, you can launch a browser by clicking on an icon or going into a special area of the online service.

7 Some online services let you use any Web browser you want to browse the World Wide Web. In that instance, you can click on an icon on the online service, go into a special area of the online service, or simply launch your Web browser on your own computer, and then begin browsing the Web.

CHAPTER

8

How ISDN Works

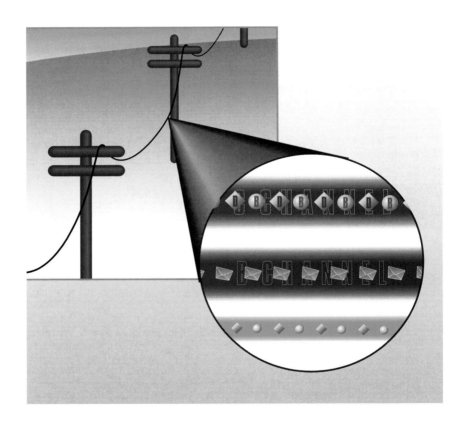

ONE common complaint about the Internet is that ordinary telephone connections are too slow. Even "high-speed" modems that can connect at 28,800 bps can be too slow to take advantage of the rich graphics now available. The Internet is full of graphics, videos, sounds, and other multimedia files which are very large, and take a very long time to be sent across the Internet to your computer.

While fiber-optic cables might eventually provide much faster data transmission, there's an affordable technology that exists today that can provide a faster Internet connection. It's called ISDN (Integrated Services Digital Network).

ISDN allows for high-speed connections to the Internet using existing copper cable telephone wires. It isn't available to everyone in the country yet because it requires that telephone companies install special ISDN digital switching equipment, although every day more areas of the country offer ISDN service. If ISDN is available in your area, you'll pay extra for the service compared to a normal telephone line.

ISDN requires that you have special equipment—something commonly referred to as an ISDN modem. Though it looks like a modem, an ISDN modem isn't really a modem at all. Instead, it's a terminal adapter, a piece of hardware that lets you send and receive digital signals over ISDN phone lines. Normal modems transform digital signals from your computer into analog signals that can be sent over normal analog telephone lines. Since ISDN is a digital technology, only digital data is sent by the ISDN adapter. Some ISDN devices include the ability to function as a regular modem. This capability is needed because not every place you can dial into with your computer lets you use ISDN; some services presently only allow regular modem access.

In order to use ISDN and the Internet, the number you're dialing will have to be equipped for ISDN access. Many private Internet dial-in providers and online services allow for ISDN access.

There are different kinds of ISDN access, but the most common one is known as *Basic Rate Interface* (*BRI*). BRI divides your telephone line into three *logical channels*. The logical channels are not separate wires, but instead are ways in which data is sent and received over your telephone lines. BRI has two 64 kbps B (*bearer*) channels, and one 16 kbps D (*data*) channel—commonly referred to as *2B+D*. The D channel sends routing information, while the two B channels send data. You can talk on one B channel while cruising the Internet on the other channel. Or, if your hardware and Internet provider or online service allows it, you can combine the two B channels into a single high-speed 128 kbps channel.

How ISDN Works

1 ISDN (Integrated Services Digital Network) is a way of establishing very high-speed connections to the Internet using existing copper telephone wires. No new telephone wires are needed in order for you to use ISDN. To allow you to use ISDN, your local telephone company will need to have installed special ISDN digital switches. Not all areas of the country have ISDN access yet. In ISDN, all the information sent between your computer and the Internet is digital.

2 In order to use ISDN service, a computer requires a special device commonly called an ISDN modem. In fact, this "modem" isn't really a modem at all, and should be called a terminal adapter instead. A normal modem (short for modulator/demodulator) converts the information inside your computer from digital into analog that can be sent over telephone lines. ISDN is a digital technology, and so there is no need to convert information from digital to analog. Instead, the ISDN "modem" sends digital information from your computer over ISDN telephone lines—and receives digital information from telephone lines.

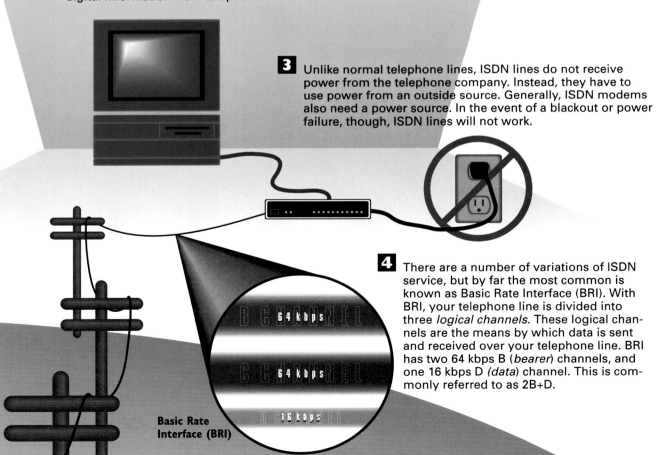

3 Unlike normal telephone lines, ISDN lines do not receive power from the telephone company. Instead, they have to use power from an outside source. Generally, ISDN modems also need a power source. In the event of a blackout or power failure, though, ISDN lines will not work.

4 There are a number of variations of ISDN service, but by far the most common is known as Basic Rate Interface (BRI). With BRI, your telephone line is divided into three *logical channels*. These logical channels are the means by which data is sent and received over your telephone line. BRI has two 64 kbps B (*bearer*) channels, and one 16 kbps D *(data)* channel. This is commonly referred to as 2B+D.

B CHANNEL **64 kbps**

C CHANNEL **64 kbps**

D CHANNEL **16 kbps**

Basic Rate Interface (BRI)

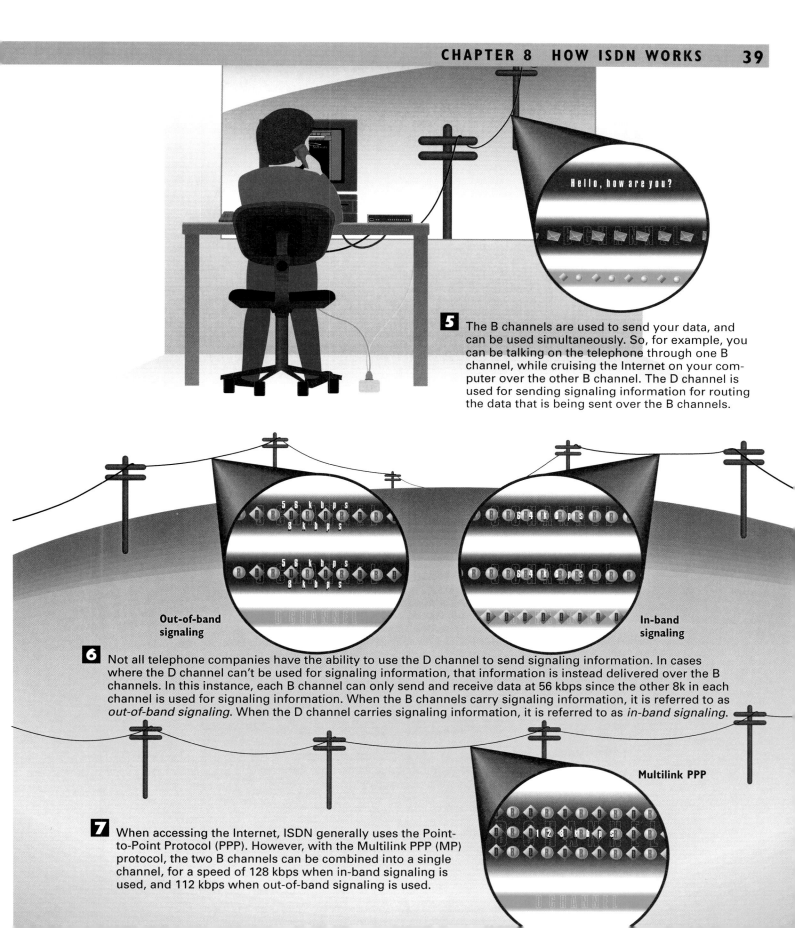

5 The B channels are used to send your data, and can be used simultaneously. So, for example, you can be talking on the telephone through one B channel, while cruising the Internet on your computer over the other B channel. The D channel is used for sending signaling information for routing the data that is being sent over the B channels.

Hello, how are you?

Out-of-band signaling

In-band signaling

6 Not all telephone companies have the ability to use the D channel to send signaling information. In cases where the D channel can't be used for signaling information, that information is instead delivered over the B channels. In this instance, each B channel can only send and receive data at 56 kbps since the other 8k in each channel is used for signaling information. When the B channels carry signaling information, it is referred to as *out-of-band signaling*. When the D channel carries signaling information, it is referred to as *in-band signaling*.

Multilink PPP

7 When accessing the Internet, ISDN generally uses the Point-to-Point Protocol (PPP). However, with the Multilink PPP (MP) protocol, the two B channels can be combined into a single channel, for a speed of 128 kbps when in-band signaling is used, and 112 kbps when out-of-band signaling is used.

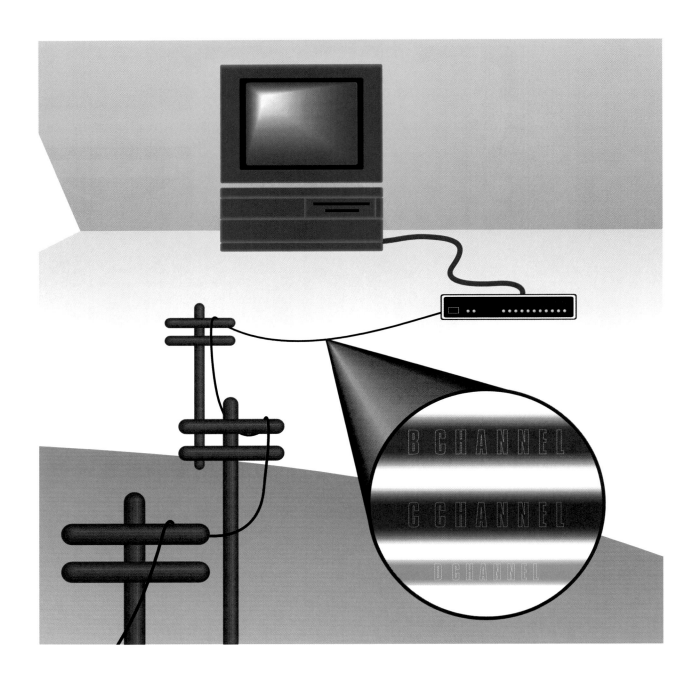

P A R T

COMMUNICATING ON THE INTERNET

FROM its very earliest days, the Internet has been primarily concerned with one task: making it easier for people to communicate with one another using computers. The Internet was created to let university researchers share their thoughts, work, and resources, and for military people to communicate with each other in case of war and even, theoretically, a nuclear attack.

Today, over two decades after the inception of the first networks that grew into the Internet, it is still primarily a communications medium. Millions of people from all over the world share their thoughts, hopes, work, gossip, and comments on the wires and computers that make up the Internet. Many of the means of communication, such as electronic mail, have changed very little in the past 20 years. Yet other entirely new ways of communicating have been devised, such as allowing you to use the Internet as your telephone, completely cutting out long-distance charges, even if you're calling to the other side of the world. There are technologies that let people communicate privately one on one, others that allow for vast discussion groups that span the globe, and still others that allow for both private communication with one person and public communications with large groups.

In this section of the book, we'll look at the main ways that people communicate on the Internet.

In Chapter 9 we'll take a long look at what continues to be the most popular way for people to communicate on the Internet—electronic mail, or e-mail. E-mail remains possibly the greatest use of the Internet, and is used for business and personal communication. We'll see how e-mail gets routed from your computer through the maze of wires that makes up the Internet, and then ends up in the proper recipient's in-box. We'll look at all the elements of a mail message, and learn how you can send binary files such as pictures and sounds through e-mail. And we'll explore mailing lists, where you can subscribe to any one of thousands of public discussions via e-mail, or can receive what are essentially electronic newsletters delivered to your e-mail in-box.

Chapter 10 explores UseNet newsgroups—public discussion groups in which anyone can participate. There are many thousands of these groups on every subject conceivable. You'll learn not just how newsgroups work, but also how you can decipher their often arcane names.

Chapter 11 covers IRC, or Internet Relay Chat. IRC is a way for people to publicly "chat" with one another on the Internet. They don't actually speak, but instead type in comments on their keyboard, and then people all over the world can read and respond to them.

Finally, Chapter 12 details one of the more intriguing new uses of the Internet: using it as your telephone. Today, you can dial into your local Internet provider with your computer, and if you have the right hardware and software, you can talk with anyone similarly connected to the Internet anywhere in the world, and all without paying long-distance telephone charges.

CHAPTER
9

How E-Mail Works

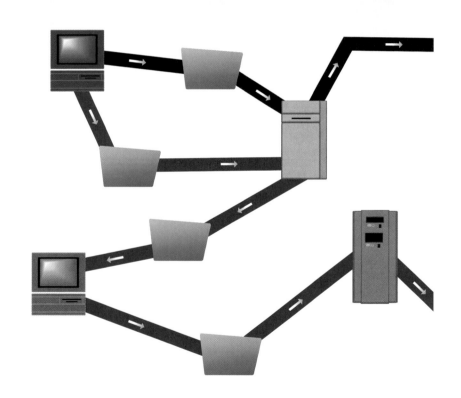

ELECTRONIC

mail, or e-mail, may be the most heavily used feature of the Internet. With it, you can send messages to anyone who is connected to the Internet, or connected to a computer network that has a connection to the Internet, such as an online service. Millions of people send and receive e-mail every day. E-mail is a great way to keep up with far-flung relatives, friends, coworkers in different branches of your company, and colleagues in your field.

E-mail messages are sent in the same way as most Internet data. The TCP protocol breaks your messages into packets, the IP protocol delivers the packets to the proper location, and then the TCP reassembles the message on the receiving end so that it can be read.

You can also attach binary files, such as pictures, videos, sounds, and executable files to your e-mail messages. Since the Internet isn't able to directly handle binary files in e-mail, the file must first be *encoded* in one of a variety of encoding schemes. Popular schemes are MIME and UUencode. The person who receives the attached binary file (called an attachment) must *decode* the file with the same scheme that was used to encode the file. Many e-mail software packages do this automatically.

When you send e-mail to someone on the Internet, that message often has to travel through a series of networks before it reaches the recipient—networks that might use different e-mail formats. *Gateways* perform the job of translating e-mail formats from one network to another so that the messages can make their way through all the networks of the Internet.

One of the most intriguing uses of e-mail is a *mailing list*. A mailing list connects a group of people who are interested in the same topic, such as Japanese cartoons or home schooling. When one person sends e-mail to the mailing list, that message is automatically sent to everyone on the list. You can meet others and talk to them on a regular basis about your shared interests, hobbies, or profession. To get onto a mailing list, you send an e-mail note to the mailing list administrator, and include your e-mail address. You cancel a subscription to the list in the same way as you subscribe to it—by sending an e-mail message to the administrator of the list.

Mailing lists can be moderated or unmoderated. A *moderated mailing list* is screened by the list administrator, who may kill duplicate messages or messages that are not related to the list's theme. An *unmoderated list* is wide open: All mail sent to it is automatically sent to everyone on the list.

Often, when you want to subscribe to a mailing list, you send a message to a computer instead of a person. That computer, known as a *list server* (also called a *listserv)* reads your e-mail and automatically subscribes you to the list. You can unsubscribe to the list in the same way. When using a list server, you have to be careful to word your request to subscribe or unsubscribe in a very precise way. If you don't, your request will be ignored, since it's read by a computer looking for certain words. If you find a mailing list you're interested in, make sure to follow the directions precisely for subscribing and unsubscribing.

Anatomy of a Mail Message

1 An e-mail message is made up of binary data, usually in the ASCII text format. ASCII is a standard that allows any computer, regardless of its operating system or hardware, to read the text. ASCII code describes the characters you see on your computer screen.

2 You can also attach pictures, executable programs, sounds, videos, and other binary files to your e-mail message. In order to do this, you'll have to encode the file in a way that will allow it to be sent across the Internet. The receiver will also have to be able to decode the file once it is received. There are a variety of different encoding schemes that can be used. Some e-mail software will automatically do the encoding for you, and also do the decoding on the receiving end.

```
0100110101011101010100110
1001000010101110101110101
0100110101011101010100110
1001000010101110101110101
0100110101011101010100110
1001000010101110101110101
0100110101011101010100110
1001000010101110101110101
0100110101011101010100110
1001000010101110101110101
0100110101011101010100110
```

```
R Y3 J K78 H E4 V K8 L9 IO
D G N5 K E3 A4 12 FO J D2
N7 S4 F43 H M5 R Y3 J
K78 H E4 V K8 L9 IO D G
N5 K E3 A4 12 FO J D2 N7
S4 F43 H M5 R Y3 J K78 H
E4 V K8 L9 IO D G N5 K E3
A4 12 FO J D2 N7 S4 F43 H
M5 R Y3 J K78 H E4 V K8
L9 IO D G N5 K E3 A4 M5
```

3 On the "To" line, type in the e-mail address of the person to whom you're sending a message. The address must be typed in following very strict rules. If you get a single letter or the syntax wrong, your message won't get to the intended recipient.

4 Your e-mail address will appear on the "From" line. Using this address, the recipient of your message will be able to respond to you.

To: gabegralla@zdnet.com
From: zlevandov@camb.com
Subject: Soccer next week

5 On the subject line, type in a very brief summary of your message.

Gabe, the soccer game next week starts at 1 pm on Saturday. Remember your cleats this time! If you need to get in touch with me, send me back e-mail.

"The mark of a great man is his friends, not his worth" – Gabie

6 At the bottom of the message is a "signature" area that can have personalized information about you. Some mail programs will automatically append this signature onto the bottom of every message you send out. Signature areas are not required and are used at the discretion of the person who creates the e-mail message. Signatures should not exceed five lines.

072105
032175
097116
101894
342714
656184
120867
122448
075431
667123
090011
124143

How E-Mail Works

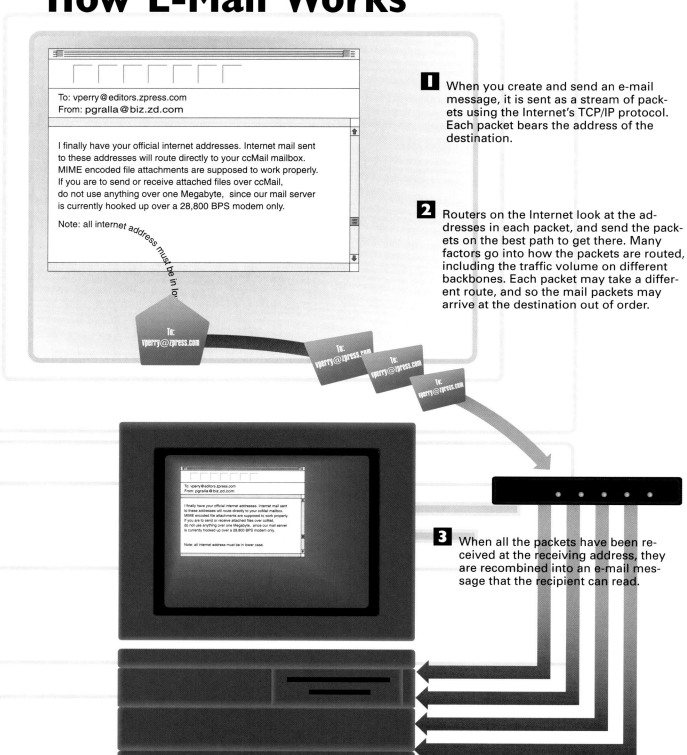

To: vperry@editors.zpress.com
From: pgralla@biz.zd.com

I finally have your official internet addresses. Internet mail sent
to these addresses will route directly to your ccMail mailbox.
MIME encoded file attachments are supposed to work properly.
If you are to send or receive attached files over ccMail,
do not use anything over one Megabyte, since our mail server
is currently hooked up over a 28,800 BPS modem only.

Note: all internet address must be in lo...

1 When you create and send an e-mail message, it is sent as a stream of packets using the Internet's TCP/IP protocol. Each packet bears the address of the destination.

2 Routers on the Internet look at the addresses in each packet, and send the packets on the best path to get there. Many factors go into how the packets are routed, including the traffic volume on different backbones. Each packet may take a different route, and so the mail packets may arrive at the destination out of order.

3 When all the packets have been received at the receiving address, they are recombined into an e-mail message that the recipient can read.

4 Using a mailing list, you can send a single message to a group of people. A *mail reflector* is the program that runs on an Internet computer and routes mail to members of a mailing list. In another kind of mailing list, known as a *listserv*, you subscribe to a mailing list by sending it your e-mail address. You will get every message that everyone sends to the list. In another kind of e-mail mailing list you can subscribe to, you only receive mail that a single person sends; only that person can send to the list. Often, electronic newsletters are distributed in this way.

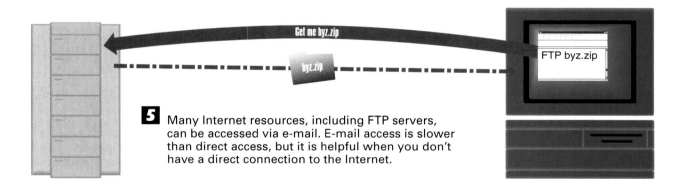

5 Many Internet resources, including FTP servers, can be accessed via e-mail. E-mail access is slower than direct access, but it is helpful when you don't have a direct connection to the Internet.

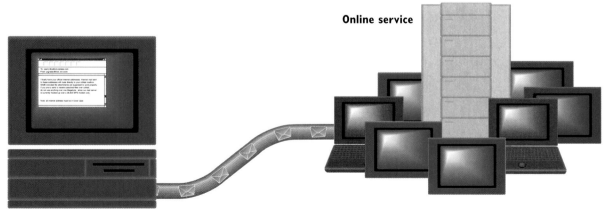

6 Using the Internet, e-mail can be exchanged between all the major online services, computer bulletin boards, and other networks. From the Internet, you can send mail to any of those networks—and from any of those networks, mail can be sent to the Internet. When mail is sent from one of those networks to another, it often must pass through the Internet as a way of routing the mail.

How E-Mail Software Works

1 When the Internet delivers mail to your e-mail box, you need some way to read the mail, compose new mail, and respond to your messages. To do all this, you'll use e-mail software, sometimes called *mailers* or *readers*.

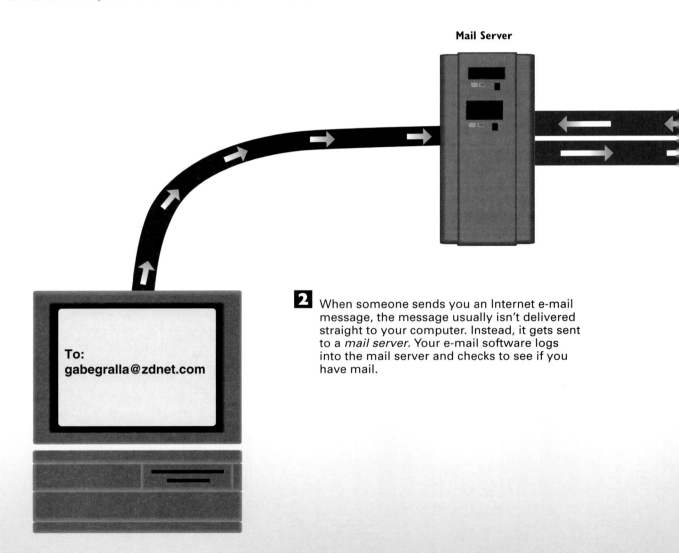

Mail Server

2 When someone sends you an Internet e-mail message, the message usually isn't delivered straight to your computer. Instead, it gets sent to a *mail server*. Your e-mail software logs into the mail server and checks to see if you have mail.

To:
gabegralla@zdnet.com

3 If you have new mail, you'll see a list of your new mail messages when you log into the server. You'll often see the name of the sender, the subject of the message, and the date and time that the message was sent.

Sender	Subject	Date ▽
News Flash	Re: Access to newsgroups f...	12/27/95 16:28 PM
Bill Jones	Re: WebWatch.	1/3/96 19:49 PM
Mary Peterson	tt#8522p Mail Server Upgra...	1/6/96 13:15 PM
Mary Peterson	FAQ: Club Member Discoun...	1/9/96 20:32 PM
Domain Names	Re: [ID-951226.578] Infor...	1/16/96 13:59 PM
info@book.com	Re: Information for book "H...	1/16/96 15:11 PM
Dave Martin	Re: [ID-951226.578] Infor...	1/17/96 19:50 PM

Do I have mail?

Here it is.

Mail Folder

- Inbox
- Trash
- Family Mail
- Mail from friends
- Office mail
- Sent mail

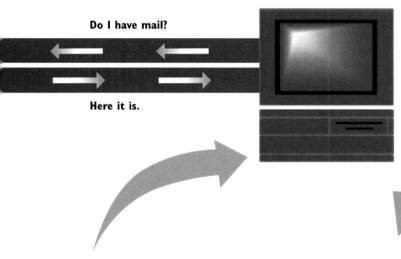

Browser - [Re: Information for book " How the Internet Works"]

File Edit Find Character Paragraph Document Help

Mail Folder	Sender	Subject	Date ▽
Inbox	Domain Names	Re: [NIC-951226.578] Infor...	1/16/96 13:59 PM
Trash	info@book	Re: Information for book "H...	1/16/96 15:11 PM
Family Mail	Dave Martin	Re: [ID-951226.578] Infor...	1/16/96 19:50 PM

Subject: Re: Information for book "How the Internet Works"
Date: Tue, 16 jan 1996 12:11:13 - 0800
From: info@book.com
To: pgralla@tiac.net

References: 1

Thank you for your recent e-mail. This message is automatically generated by our server as we are overwhelmed by the number of responses we received. Nevertheless, we look forward to seeing your book in print.

5 E-mail software lets you do things such as create folders for storing mail, allow you to search through your messages, keep an address book of people to whom you send mail, create group mailing lists, create and add a signature file, and more.

4 When you want to read a mail message, you tell your software to download it to your own computer. There, you read the message using your mail reader, and you can file it, delete it, or respond to it.

How a Mailing List Works

Mailing lists are a way for groups of people to have public discussions carried on via e-mail. When you join a mailing list, every message you write to the list can be read by everyone on the list.

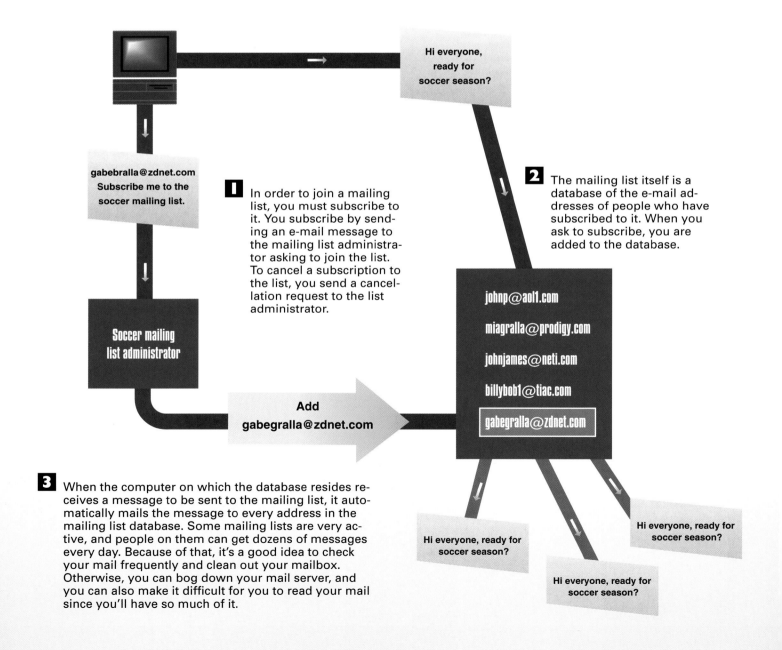

1 In order to join a mailing list, you must subscribe to it. You subscribe by sending an e-mail message to the mailing list administrator asking to join the list. To cancel a subscription to the list, you send a cancellation request to the list administrator.

2 The mailing list itself is a database of the e-mail addresses of people who have subscribed to it. When you ask to subscribe, you are added to the database.

3 When the computer on which the database resides receives a message to be sent to the mailing list, it automatically mails the message to every address in the mailing list database. Some mailing lists are very active, and people on them can get dozens of messages every day. Because of that, it's a good idea to check your mail frequently and clean out your mailbox. Otherwise, you can bog down your mail server, and you can also make it difficult for you to read your mail since you'll have so much of it.

How E-Mail Is Sent between Networks

Internet e-mail can easily be sent between networks on the Internet, or between online services such as CompuServe and America Online, via the Internet. Here are all the steps a typical message might go through while being sent from one network to another.

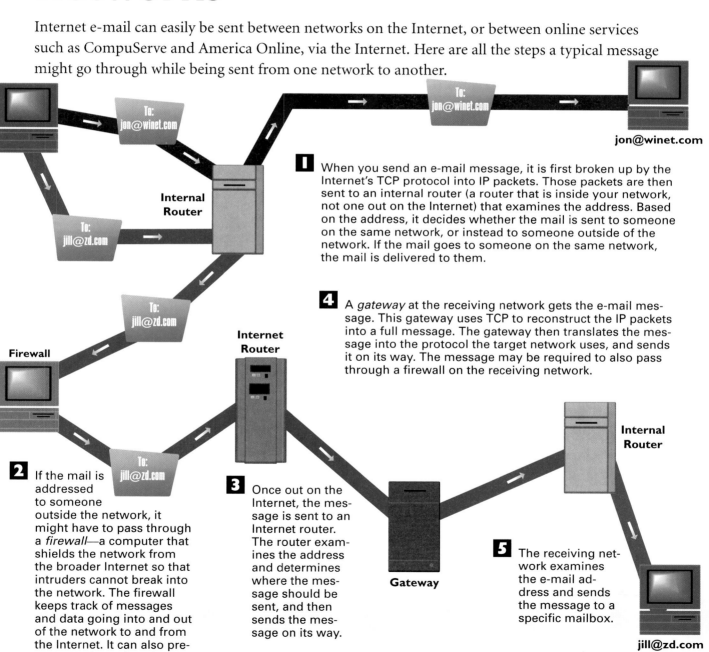

Internal Router

jon@winet.com

1 When you send an e-mail message, it is first broken up by the Internet's TCP protocol into IP packets. Those packets are then sent to an internal router (a router that is inside your network, not one out on the Internet) that examines the address. Based on the address, it decides whether the mail is sent to someone on the same network, or instead to someone outside of the network. If the mail goes to someone on the same network, the mail is delivered to them.

4 A *gateway* at the receiving network gets the e-mail message. This gateway uses TCP to reconstruct the IP packets into a full message. The gateway then translates the message into the protocol the target network uses, and sends it on its way. The message may be required to also pass through a firewall on the receiving network.

Internet Router

Firewall

Internal Router

2 If the mail is addressed to someone outside the network, it might have to pass through a *firewall*—a computer that shields the network from the broader Internet so that intruders cannot break into the network. The firewall keeps track of messages and data going into and out of the network to and from the Internet. It can also prevent certain packets from getting through it.

3 Once out on the Internet, the message is sent to an Internet router. The router examines the address and determines where the message should be sent, and then sends the message on its way.

Gateway

5 The receiving network examines the e-mail address and sends the message to a specific mailbox.

jill@zd.com

CHAPTER

10

How UseNet Newsgroups Work

USENET,

the world's biggest electronic discussion forum, provides a way for messages to be sent among computers across the entire Internet. People from all over the world participate in discussions on many thousands of topics, in specific areas of interest called *newsgroups.*

There are at least 20 different major hierarchies of newsgroups, such as recreation (identified by the letters "rec"), and computers (identified by the letters "comp"). Within these major hierarchies are subcategories (such as rec.arts) and further subcategories (such as rec.arts.books). Individual newsgroups can cover anything from movies to parenting, ecology, sports teams, clip art, and news about UseNet itself. Not all Internet sites carry all newsgroups. An administrator at each site decides which newsgroups to carry.

To participate in newsgroups, you'll need special software to read and respond to them. There are readers for PC, Macintosh, and UNIX computers. Online services such as CompuServe and America Online have their own proprietary software that lets you participate in newsgroups.

A good newsgroup reader will let you view the ongoing discussions as threads. *Threads* are ongoing conversations that are grouped by topic. So, for example, in the rec.arts.books newsgroup there may be many different threads going on at one time, each discussing a different book.

Many newsgroups have a list of Frequently Asked Questions, or FAQs, (pronounced "facks") associated with them. These FAQs answer common questions about the newsgroup. It's a good idea to read the FAQ before submitting questions to the newsgroup as a whole.

You participate in newsgroups by reading the messages and responding to them. There are moderated and unmoderated newsgroups. In a moderated newsgroup, each message goes to a human moderator. The moderator looks at the messages, making sure they're appropriate for the group. If they are appropriate, the messages are posted. All messages sent to an unmoderated newsgroup are automatically posted.

When messages are posted, UseNet servers distribute them to other sites that carry the newsgroup. A site usually carries only the most current messages—otherwise they would soon run out of storage space. Some sites *archive*, or store, old discussions.

A convenient way to check newsgroups is to *subscribe* to those that you are interested in. That way, whenever you check the UseNet server, new messages in your subscribed newsgroup will be delivered to you. You can also cancel your subscription to a newsgroup if you are no longer interested in it. You can read newsgroups without subscribing to them; in that case you'll have to manually ask to read specific newsgroups instead of having it done automatically for you.

Binary files such as pictures and multimedia can be posted in newsgroups. These files must be specially encoded in order for them to be posted. In order to view them, you'll have to transfer them to your computer, and then unencode them with special software. A common encoding scheme used on newsgroups is called UUencode.

How UseNet Works

1 UseNet is a global bulletin board and discussion area. It collects messages about many thousands of different topics into newsgroups—freewheeling discussion areas in which anyone can participate. Newsgroups can be found on many host computers across the Internet. There are thousands of newsgroups that cover just about every topic you've ever imagined—and many you probably haven't.

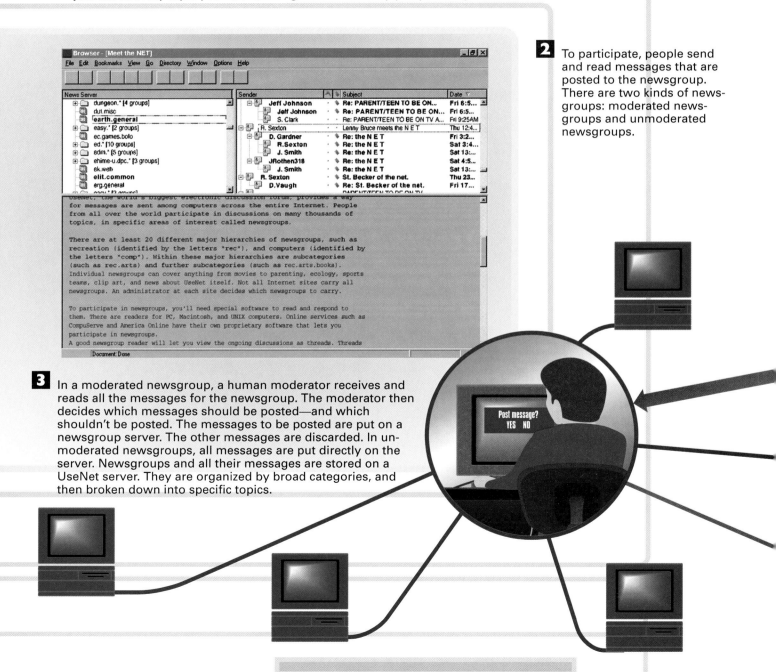

2 To participate, people send and read messages that are posted to the newsgroup. There are two kinds of newsgroups: moderated newsgroups and unmoderated newsgroups.

3 In a moderated newsgroup, a human moderator receives and reads all the messages for the newsgroup. The moderator then decides which messages should be posted—and which shouldn't be posted. The messages to be posted are put on a newsgroup server. The other messages are discarded. In unmoderated newsgroups, all messages are put directly on the server. Newsgroups and all their messages are stored on a UseNet server. They are organized by broad categories, and then broken down into specific topics.

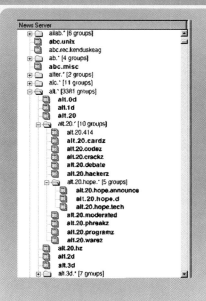

6 Newsgroup reader software lets you read messages and respond to newsgroups. The software gives you ways to manage your newsgroups by also allowing you to subscribe to newsgroups, which means that new messages will automatically be delivered to you when you check the server. You'll also be able to cancel your subscription.

5 Pictures, multimedia files, and even executable programs can be posted in newsgroups for other people to see and use. However, because of the technology used in newsgroups, those files must be specially encoded in order for them to be posted. In order to view, play, or use the files, you'll have to first transfer them to your own computer, and then unencode them with special software. A common encoding scheme used on newsgroups is called UUencode. There are versions of this encoding and decoding program that work on PC, Macintosh, and UNIX computers.

"Check out this picture"

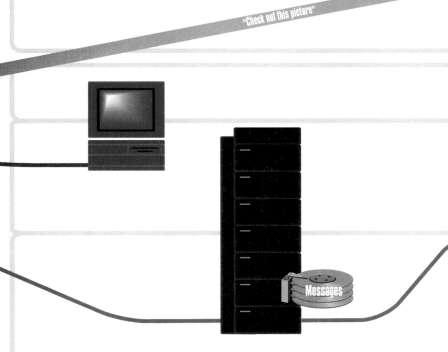

4 UseNet servers communicate with one another so that all messages posted on one server are duplicated on the other servers. While there are many UseNet servers, not all servers carry all newsgroups. Each site decides which newsgroups to carry.

Understanding the Hierarchy of UseNet Newsgroups

1 There are thousands of UseNet newsgroups. They are divided into hierarchies of topics to make it easier for you to find the particular newsgroups you want to participate in. Not all sites carry all newsgroups. System administrators decide which newsgroups to carry at their site. Online services, as well as Internet providers that give direct connections to the Internet, allow access to UseNet newsgroups.

2 In the hierarchy of UseNet newsgroups, the major topic (such as "rec" for recreation) comes first, followed by a subtopic (such as "rec.arts"). That subtopic can be further subdivided (such as "rec.arts.books"), and then subdivided even further, if need be. Pictured in this illustration are many of the major newsgroup topics, but they are only a very tiny percentage of the total number of the thousands of newsgroups available. New newsgroups are constantly being created, and old ones are constantly being eliminated.

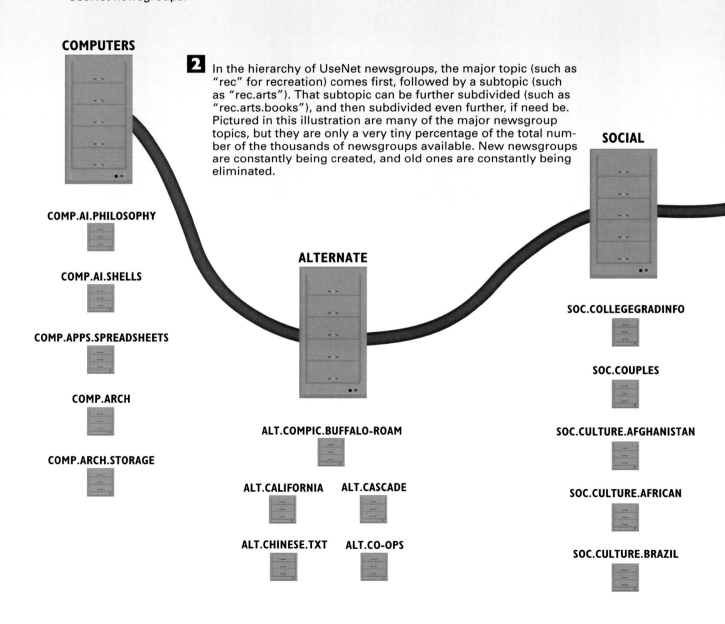

COMPUTERS

COMP.AI.PHILOSOPHY

COMP.AI.SHELLS

COMP.APPS.SPREADSHEETS

COMP.ARCH

COMP.ARCH.STORAGE

ALTERNATE

ALT.COMPIC.BUFFALO-ROAM

ALT.CALIFORNIA   ALT.CASCADE

ALT.CHINESE.TXT   ALT.CO-OPS

SOCIAL

SOC.COLLEGEGRADINFO

SOC.COUPLES

SOC.CULTURE.AFGHANISTAN

SOC.CULTURE.AFRICAN

SOC.CULTURE.BRAZIL

3 You can often tell what the newsgroup is by its name. Major UseNet topics include "comp" for discussions of computer-related topics; "soc" for discussions of societal topics; "sci" for discussions of scientific topics; "news" for discussions about newsgroups; "rec" for discussions of recreation topics; and "alt" for discussion of "alternate" topics, among others. So, for example, the rec.arts.books newsgroup carries discussion about books.

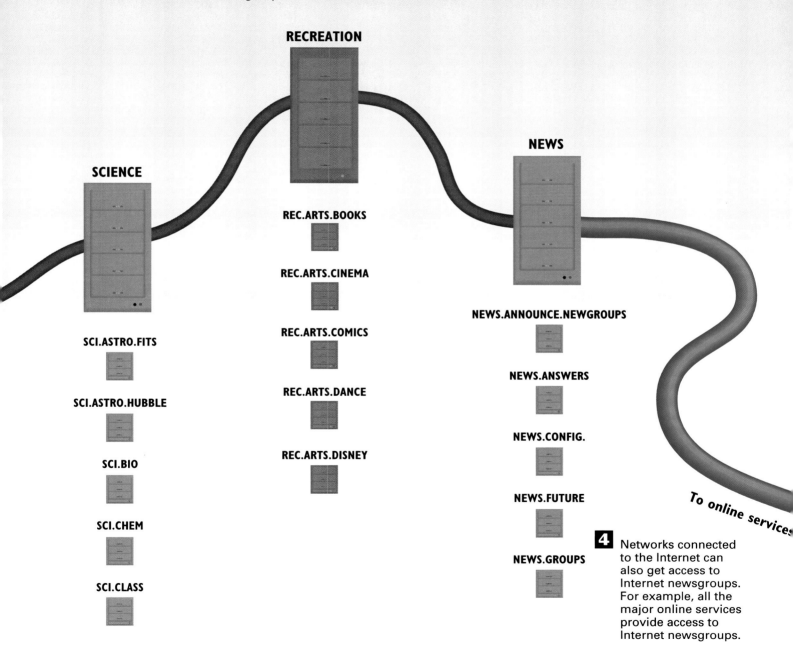

RECREATION

NEWS

SCIENCE

REC.ARTS.BOOKS

REC.ARTS.CINEMA

REC.ARTS.COMICS

REC.ARTS.DANCE

REC.ARTS.DISNEY

NEWS.ANNOUNCE.NEWGROUPS

NEWS.ANSWERS

NEWS.CONFIG.

NEWS.FUTURE

NEWS.GROUPS

SCI.ASTRO.FITS

SCI.ASTRO.HUBBLE

SCI.BIO

SCI.CHEM

SCI.CLASS

To online services

4 Networks connected to the Internet can also get access to Internet newsgroups. For example, all the major online services provide access to Internet newsgroups.

CHAPTER

11

How Internet Relay Chat Works

ONE of the most immediate ways to communicate with others via the Internet is to participate in live "chat." Internet Relay Chat doesn't refer to people actually talking to each other and hearing each other's voices. Instead, it means that you hold live keyboard "conversations" with other people on the Internet—that is, you type words on your computer and other people on the Internet can see those words on their computer immediately, and vice versa. You can hold chats with many people simultaneously all over the world.

There are a number of ways to chat on the Internet, but the most popular one is called IRC, or Internet Relay Chat. Every day, thousands of people all over the world hold conversations via IRC on many different topics. Each different topic is called a "channel." When you join a channel, you can see what everyone else on the channel types on their keyboard. In turn, whatever you type on your keyboard can be seen by everyone in the channel. You can also hold individual side conversations with someone.

IRC has facilitated communications during natural disasters, wars, and other crises. In 1993, for example, during the attempted Communist coup in Russia when Russian legislators barricaded themselves inside the Parliament building, an IRC "news channel" was set up for relaying real-time, first-person accounts of the events taking place. And during the 1994 Los Angeles earthquake, a special channel was set up to relay information related to the earthquake. It has also been used during hurricanes and other natural disasters.

IRC follows a client-server model, which means that both client and server software are required in order to use it. There are many IRC clients for many different kinds of computers, so whether you have a PC, a Macintosh, or a UNIX workstation, you'll be able to use IRC.

Your IRC client communicates with an IRC server on the Internet. You log into a server using the client and pick a channel on which you want to chat. When you type words on your keyboard, they are sent to your server. Your server is part of a global IRC server network connected in a spanning tree structure—each server is connected to several other servers in a tree-like manner; they do not all directly connect to one another. Your server sends your message to other servers, which sends your messages to people who are part of your channel. They can then see and respond to your message.

How IRC Works

1 IRC (Internet Relay Chat) is a way for people all over the world to "chat" with one another by typing commands on their keyboards. The words you type are instantly relayed to people's computers all over the world, where they can read them. You in turn can read what other people are typing in their computers. All this happens in "real time"—you see the words as people type them.

2 IRC runs on a client/server model, which means that in order to use it, you need client software on your computer. There are many IRC clients available for PCs, Macintoshes, UNIX workstations, and many other kinds of computers.

3 When you want to chat, you make a connection to the Internet, and then start your client software. Then you need to log into an IRC server located on the Internet. There are many IRC servers located all over the world. They are connected together in a network so that they can send messages to one another. The servers are connected in a "spanning tree" fashion in which each server is connected to several others, but all the servers are not directly connected to one another.

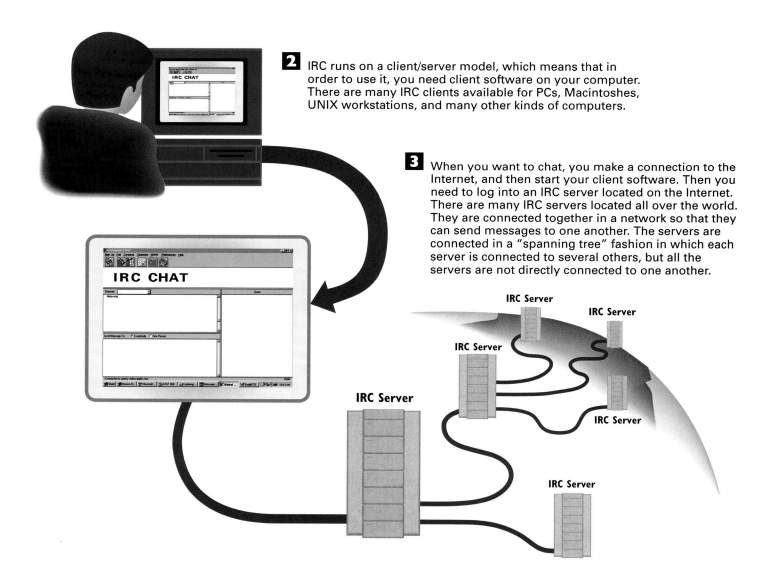

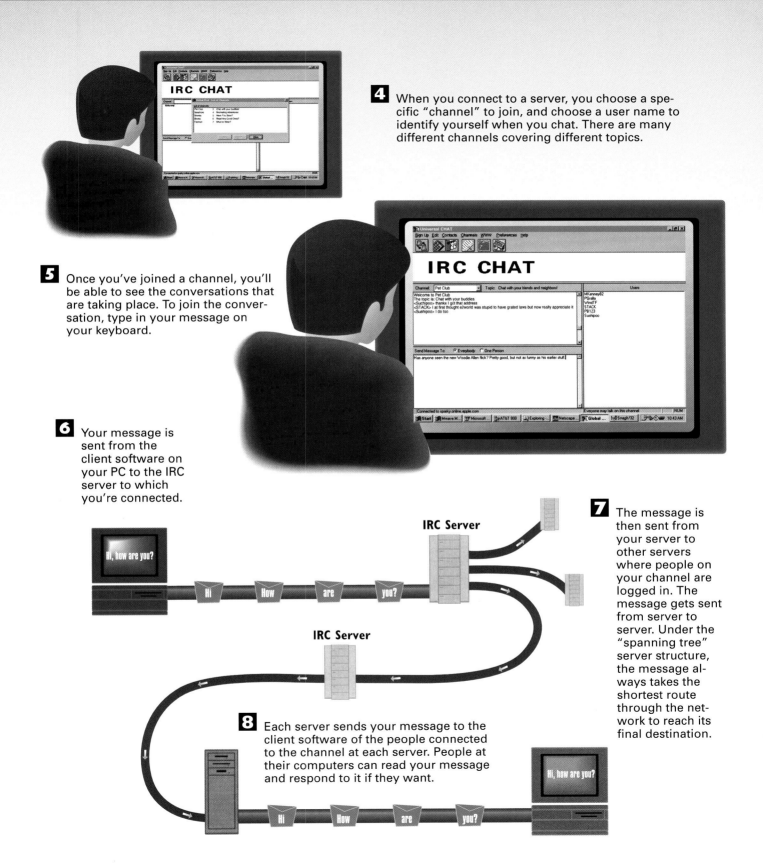

4 When you connect to a server, you choose a specific "channel" to join, and choose a user name to identify yourself when you chat. There are many different channels covering different topics.

5 Once you've joined a channel, you'll be able to see the conversations that are taking place. To join the conversation, type in your message on your keyboard.

6 Your message is sent from the client software on your PC to the IRC server to which you're connected.

IRC Server

7 The message is then sent from your server to other servers where people on your channel are logged in. The message gets sent from server to server. Under the "spanning tree" server structure, the message always takes the shortest route through the network to reach its final destination.

IRC Server

8 Each server sends your message to the client software of the people connected to the channel at each server. People at their computers can read your message and respond to it if they want.

Hi, how are you?

C H A P T E R

12

Making Phone Calls on the Internet

T HE Internet has pioneered many new ways to communicate, such as e-mail, live chat, and newsgroups. But it can also be used to enable some old-fashioned communications as well: You can make telephone calls using the Internet. The revolutionary part of using the Internet to make phone calls is the price: It's free. You only pay for your Internet connection, as if you were browsing the Web or sending e-mail. You don't actually have to pay for the phone call itself. And you can make calls anywhere in the world—you can call Tokyo just as easily as you can call someone in your town, and you won't have to pay a penny more.

There are many different schemes and software packages that will allow you to make phone calls on the Internet. With them, you don't actually use your telephone. Instead, you speak into a microphone attached to your computer, and listen through speakers and a sound card.

You will only be able to make telephone calls to and receive calls from someone who has an Internet address, so you won't be able to replace your telephone by using the Internet. There are a number of different competing products that let you talk over the Internet—but as of yet they don't communicate with one another. There is no standard way of making telephone calls, so that means you'll only be able to talk to people who use the exact same software you do for making and receiving phone calls.

Many companies make software designed to let you make phone calls over the Internet: NetPhone from Electric Magic, WebTalk from Quarterdeck, WebPhone from the Internet Telephone Company, and Internet Phone from VocalTec are just a few.

Although each company's software works somewhat differently, in general they use similar ways of letting people make phone calls over the Internet. In order to make a phone call, you'll have to first know someone's Internet address. You will, however, be able to consult directories which function like telephone books.

Once you find out the person's Internet address, you can connect to them by running special software, and then by double-clicking on their name. A message goes out to them over the Internet to see if they're available to talk.

While the number of people to whom you can make phone calls today is relatively small, that number will grow. Even today the technology is useful for friends, family, and business associates who often make phone calls to each other, because they can use the same software, and then save significant amounts of money on their telephone bills.

How to Make Phone Calls Using the Internet

There are many different technologies and ways to use the Internet to make telephone calls. This page describes making phone calls through the Internet with the WebTalk technology from Quarterdeck.

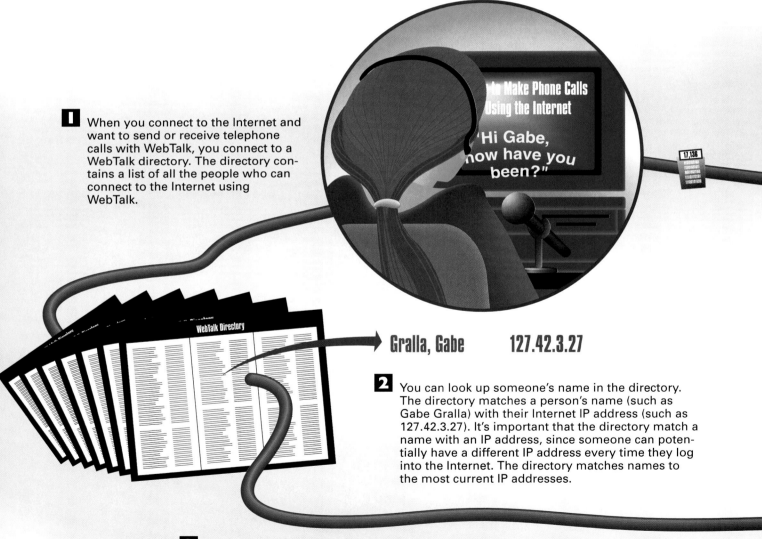

1 When you connect to the Internet and want to send or receive telephone calls with WebTalk, you connect to a WebTalk directory. The directory contains a list of all the people who can connect to the Internet using WebTalk.

Gralla, Gabe   127.42.3.27

2 You can look up someone's name in the directory. The directory matches a person's name (such as Gabe Gralla) with their Internet IP address (such as 127.42.3.27). It's important that the directory match a name with an IP address, since someone can potentially have a different IP address every time they log into the Internet. The directory matches names to the most current IP addresses.

3 When you find someone in the directory you want to call, the directory looks up their IP address, and then routes your call directly to their computer. The "phone" "rings" at the person's computer. They pick up the receiver. The two of you can now talk using the sound cards and microphones attached to your computers.

"Hi Gabe, how have you been?"

4 When you talk into the microphone, software turns your voice into binary data files that can be read by computers. It also compresses the voice data to make it smaller and able to be sent over the Internet more quickly. Normally, voice files are very large, and without compression would be too large to quickly send over the Internet.

5 The software also determines the speed of the Internet connection. If the connection is a high-speed connection, it creates voice files of high quality. If it's a lower-speed connection, it creates files of a lesser sound quality, because at lower speeds, it would take too long to send voice files, even after they've been compressed.

HI GABE, HOW HAVE YOU BEEN?

28,800 bps

H I G A B E , H O W H A

14,400 bps

5,485

2,578

1,358

5,924

6 The software breaks up the voice files into a series of packets to be sent over the Internet using the Internet's TCP/IP protocols.

6,257

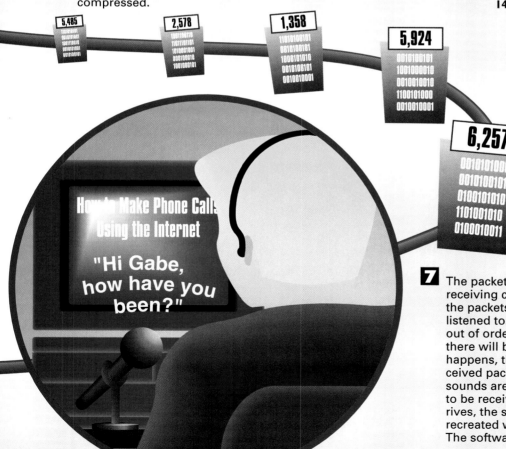

7 The packets are sent to the receiver. On the receiving computer, software decompresses the packets so that they can be played and listened to. Sometimes, packets will arrive out of order on the receiving end, and so there will be missing packets. When that happens, the software, based on the received packets, is able to estimate what the sounds are in the missing packet that has yet to be received. When the missing packet arrives, the software knows that it has already recreated what it would have sounded like. The software will then discard the packet.

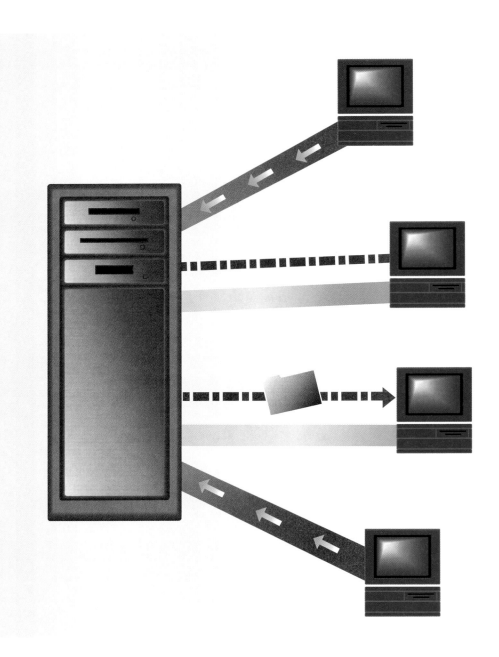

P A R T

COMMON INTERNET TOOLS

THERE'S an enormous amount of information and entertainment on the Internet, but how do you get access to it? It's not quite as simple as turning on your television or reading your daily newspaper.

The solution is to use a variety of Internet tools. These tools let you tap into the colossal resources of the Internet. Some of these resources, such as the World Wide Web, are quite well known. Others, such as WAIS (wide area information server), are not nearly as popular. In this section, we'll look at how the most common and useful Internet tools work.

In Chapter 13 we'll take a look at the fastest growing and most visible part of the Internet—the World Wide Web. To a great degree, the explosive growth of the Web is what's fueled the enormous amount of interest in the Internet in the last several years. We'll learn what the Web is, how a Web browser works, and investigate in detail what URLs (universal resource locators) are.

Chapter 14 details how a *gopher* works. A gopher was one of the first attempts to corral the enormous amount of information available on the Internet. It helps solve a major problem with the Internet—there's so much information, it can be difficult to find what you want. Gophers work on a simple menuing system, and allow you to access information no matter where it's found, without having to remember to launch other Internet resources such as FTP (file transfer protocol) or Telnet.

Chapter 15 covers one of the older Internet technologies, and one which is still in widespread use—Telnet. Telnet allows you to take over the resources of a distant computer while sitting at your own computer. What you type on your keyboard is sent across the Internet to the distant computer, the commands are carried out by the distant computer, and the results of your commands are sent to your own computer screen. It appears as if you're sitting at the distant computer's keyboard. There are many different uses for Telnet, notably libraries making their catalogs available over the Internet. When you log into a distant computer using Telnet, you often use a menuing system.

In Chapter 16 we'll take a close look at one of the lesser-known Internet resources—WAIS. Through WAIS, you can search many databases located on the Internet, often using plain English search commands. And WAIS also allows you to do relevancy searching; you can ask WAIS to find documents for you that are related to a particular document you've found that you're interested in.

Finally, in Chapter 17 we'll cover one of the most popular uses of the Internet—downloading files. Generally, files are downloaded from the Internet using the Internet protocol FTP. We'll look not only at how FTP works, but also at how files are compressed and uncompressed on the Internet. A compressed file will take less time to be sent over the Internet to your computer.

CHAPTER

13

How the World Wide Web Works

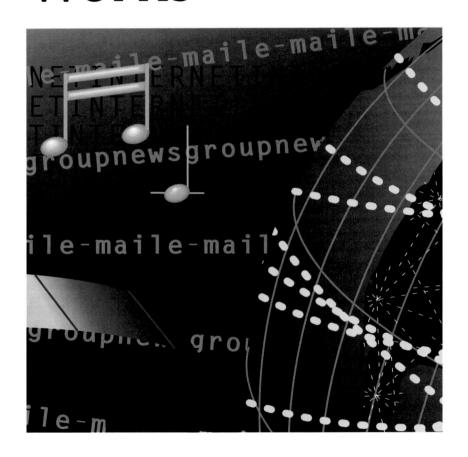

THE World Wide Web is the fastest growing and in many ways the most exciting and intriguing part of the Internet. When people refer to "surfing the Net," more often than not they're talking about using the World Wide Web.

As its name implies, the World Wide Web is a globally connected network. The Web contains many things, but what makes it so fascinating to so many are the *home pages* that incorporate text, graphics, sound, animation, and other multimedia elements. In essence, each home page is an interactive multimedia publication.

Home pages are connected to each other using *hypertext* that allows you to move from any home page to any other home page, and to graphics, binary files, multimedia files, and any Internet resource. To jump from one home page to another, you merely click on a hypertext link. The same holds true for other Internet resources such as multimedia files, newsgroups, and other resources—to get access to them, you merely click on a link on a home page.

The Web operates on a client/server model. You run a Web client on your computer—called a Web browser—such as Mosaic, Netscape, or the Internet Explorer. That client contacts a Web server and requests information or resources. The Web server locates and then sends the information to the Web browser, which displays the results.

Home pages on the Web are built using a markup language called HTML (Hypertext Markup Language). The language contains commands that tell your browser how to display text, graphics, and multimedia files. It also contains commands for linking the home page to other home pages, and to other Internet resources.

Sometimes, home pages contain links to files that the Web browser can't play or display, such as sound or animation files. In that case, you'll need a *helper application.* You configure your Web browser to use the helper application whenever it comes across a sound or animation file that the browser itself can't run or play.

Many Web pages appear quite complex. In fact, though, Web pages can be simple to build—with the right tools. The major online services include tools to let you build and post your own home pages. There are also many different kinds of software that will let you create your own home pages. With a little effort, you can become a worldwide publisher, and can participate in the Web instead of just being an observer.

How the World Wide Web Works

1 The World Wide Web is the fastest growing and most innovative part of the Internet. When you browse the Web, you view multimedia home pages composed of text, graphics, and multimedia contents such as sound and video. The Web uses *hypertext links* that allow you to jump from any place on the Web to any other place on the Web. The language that allows you to use hypertext links and to view Web pages is called Hypertext Markup Language, more commonly known as HTML.

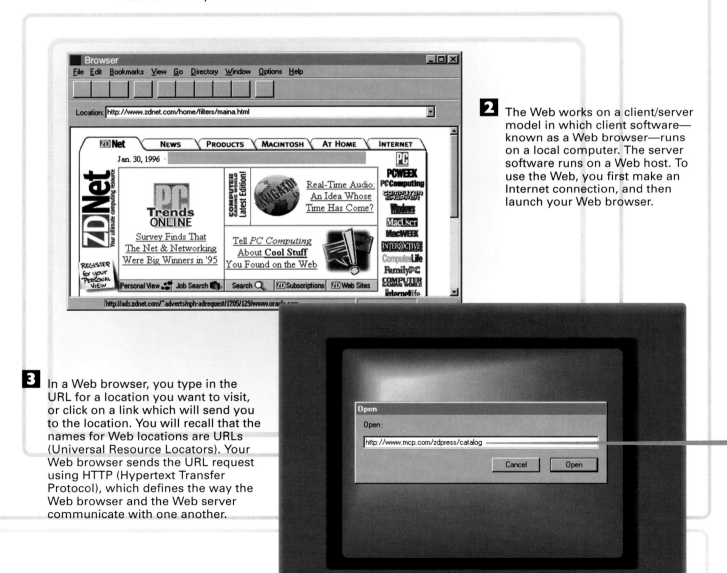

2 The Web works on a client/server model in which client software—known as a Web browser—runs on a local computer. The server software runs on a Web host. To use the Web, you first make an Internet connection, and then launch your Web browser.

3 In a Web browser, you type in the URL for a location you want to visit, or click on a link which will send you to the location. You will recall that the names for Web locations are URLs (Universal Resource Locators). Your Web browser sends the URL request using HTTP (Hypertext Transfer Protocol), which defines the way the Web browser and the Web server communicate with one another.

7 When the server finds the requested home page, document, or object, it sends that home page, document, or object back to the Web browser client. The information is now displayed on the computer screen in the Web browser. When the page is sent from the server, the http connection is closed, and can be reopened.

www.mcp.com/zdpress.catalog

6 The Web server receives the request using the http protocol. It is told which specific document is being requested.

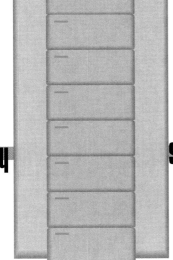

ssərdpz/woɔ·dɔw·www//:dʇʇɥ ɓolɐʇɐɔ·ssərd

5 The request is sent to the Internet. Internet routers examine the request to determine which server to send the request to. The information just to the right of the "http://" in the URL tells the Internet on which Web server the requested information can be found. Routers send the request to that Web server.

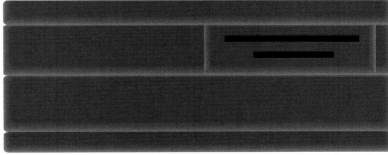

http://www.mcp.com/zdpress.catalog

4 URLs contain several parts. The first part—the "http://"—details what Internet protocol to use. The second part—the part that usually has a "www" in it—sometimes tells what kind of Internet resource is being contacted. The third part—such as "zdnet.com"—can vary in length, and identifies the Web server to be contacted. The final part identifies a specific directory on the server, and a home page, document, or other Internet object.

How a Web Browser Works

1 Web browsers are client software that runs on your computer and displays Web home pages. There are clients for PC, Macintosh, and UNIX computers.

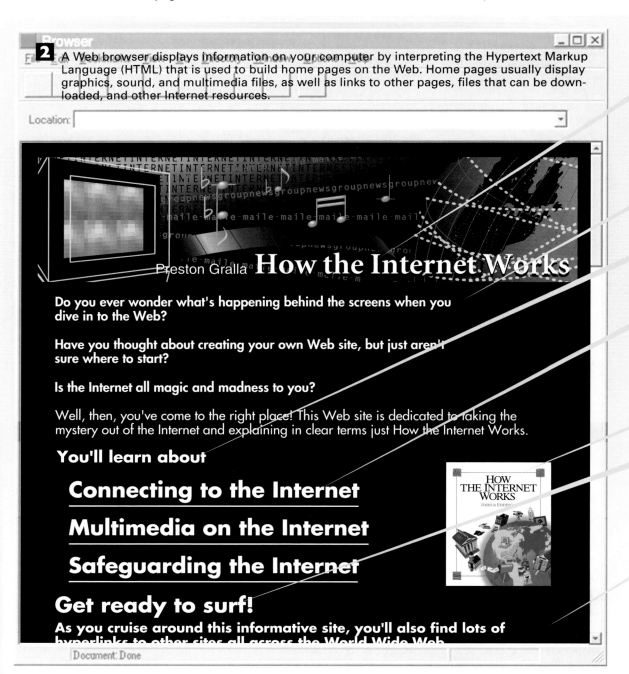

2 A Web browser displays information on your computer by interpreting the Hypertext Markup Language (HTML) that is used to build home pages on the Web. Home pages usually display graphics, sound, and multimedia files, as well as links to other pages, files that can be downloaded, and other Internet resources.

Location:

Preston Gralla **How the Internet Works**

Do you ever wonder what's happening behind the screens when you dive in to the Web?

Have you thought about creating your own Web site, but just aren't sure where to start?

Is the Internet all magic and madness to you?

Well, then, you've come to the right place! This Web site is dedicated to taking the mystery out of the Internet and explaining in clear terms just How the Internet Works.

You'll learn about

Connecting to the Internet

Multimedia on the Internet

Safeguarding the Internet

Get ready to surf!

As you cruise around this informative site, you'll also find lots of hyperlinks to other sites all across the World Wide Web.

HOW THE INTERNET WORKS
JOSHUA EDDING

Document: Done

```
<HTML>
<HEAD>
<TITLE>
</HEAD>
```

3 The coding in the HTML files tells your browser how to display the text, graphics, links, and multimedia files on the home page. The HTML file that your browser loads to display the home page doesn't actually have the graphics, sound, multimedia files and other resources on it. Instead, it contains HTML references to those graphics and files. Your browser uses those references to find the files on the server, and then display them on the home page.

```
<BODY>
<P> Do you ever wonder what's happening behind
the screens when you dive in to the Web?

<H3> You'll learn about:

<A HREF="URL"> Go TO URL</A>
```

4 The Web browser also interprets HTML tags as links to other Web sites, or to other Web resources, such as graphics, multimedia files, newsgroups, or files to download. Depending on the link, it will perform different actions. For example, if the HTML code specifies the link as another home page, the browser will retrieve the URL specified in the HTML file when the user clicks on the underlined link on the page. If the HTML code specifies a file to be downloaded, the browser will download the file to your computer.

```
<P> <IMG SRC="BOOK.GIF"

<H2> Get ready to surf!

<P> As you cruise around this informative site,
you'll also find lots of hyperlinks to other sites all
across the World Wide Web.

</BODY>
<HTML>
```

NOTE There are many different kinds of files on the Internet that Web browsers themselves cannot display, particularly many kinds of multimedia files such as sound, video, and animation files. Still, there are often references to these kinds of files on Web pages. In order to view or play these files, you'll need what are called "helper applications." You configure your Web browser to launch these helper applications whenever you click on an object that needs them in order to be viewed. Helper applications can also be used for displaying virtual reality pages, for chatting on the Internet, and to do other Internet tasks.

NOTE The meanings of tags are easily decipherable. Every HTML tag, or instruction, is surrounded by a less-than and a greater-than sign: <P>. Often tags appear in pairs, the beginning tag and the ending tag. They are identical except for a simple slash in the end tag. So a paragraph of text will frequently be surrounded by tags like this: <P> Paragraph of text.</P>. Also, tags are not case sensitive. <P> equals <p>.

CHAPTER

14

How Gophers Work

To a certain extent, the Internet has been a victim of its success. There is such an enormous amount of information on it that it's often difficult to find what you want.

This problem led to the development of a software program called an Internet gopher. A gopher organizes information in a logical, hierarchical, tree-like fashion to lead you to files, Internet resources, data, and anything else you might search for on the Internet. Gophers were the first client software programs to allow access to many types of protocols and servers from within one client.

Because gophers make it easy to access many types of information, they helped fuel the Internet's growth. Since they are easy to build, they set in motion a wave of publishing on the Internet. They are not used as frequently now as they were in early days, however.

There are many gophers located on the Internet. Organizations and universities generally create gophers, often for internal use by employees or students. Most of the gophers you'll come across are created and maintained by universities, and have been set up as a way to make it easier for students to tap into the resources of the university and the Internet. Though the gophers were created by the university or an organization, they are often made available to anyone on the Internet.

Gophers work in a client/server model. You run a gopher client on your own computer. The client sends requests to a gopher server located on the Internet. The server sends back the information to the client, which displays the information on your computer screen. There are gopher clients available for PCs, Macintoshes, and UNIX computers. Online services also have gopher client software built into them.

Gophers are organized in a tree-like menu fashion. When you first engage a gopher, you'll be greeted with the gopher's main menu, called the *root gopher*. From this menu you choose items that you're interested in. Frequently, those items will be other menus, called sub-menus. Keep burrowing down through menus until you reach the information you want.

Gophers can link you to many types of Internet resources. They can lead you to text files, binary files, log-ins to remote computers, graphics files, multimedia files, and WAIS database searches, among other resources. What's helpful about gophers is that you won't need to know which kind of Internet resource is required to get the information—a gopher takes care of it for you. For example, if you request a file through a gopher, the gopher will automatically send it through FTP to your computer; you don't need to launch FTP software. And if the gopher leads you to log in to a remote computer, the gopher will do it for you; you won't need to launch a separate Telnet session.

How a Gopher Works

A gopher is an Internet resource that organizes information and files in a hierarchical, tree-like order. It features a simple-to-use menuing system to let you find information without needing to know the information's IP address or domain name. Gophers can organize many kinds of information, including text files, binary files, graphics files, and multimedia files. Gophers can also link you to many Internet resources such as other gophers, WAIS database searches, and logins to distant computers using Telnet. The information you request often doesn't reside on the gopher. Instead, the gopher points you to other locations on the Internet.

1 A gopher follows the client/server model. The gopher client sends requests to the gopher server, which then sends back the requested information to the client. The client then displays the information on your computer. You can use special gopher client software or a Web browser, which has the ability to function as a gopher client. Online services have their own built-in gopher clients. If you don't have a Web browser or gopher client software, you can use Telnet to go to a public gopher on the Internet. No matter how you access gophers, though, they will generally work the same.

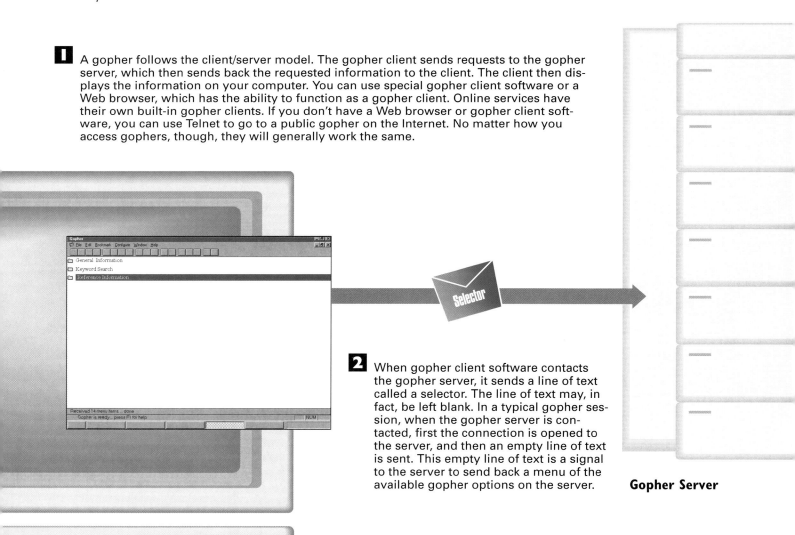

2 When gopher client software contacts the gopher server, it sends a line of text called a selector. The line of text may, in fact, be left blank. In a typical gopher session, when the gopher server is contacted, first the connection is opened to the server, and then an empty line of text is sent. This empty line of text is a signal to the server to send back a menu of the available gopher options on the server.

Gopher Server

User Display String

Selector String

3 The server sends a series of lines back to the client, each of which ends with a carriage return and line feed. Each line is made up of a series of components separated by tab characters: a number; text called a *user display string* that the gopher user will see in a menu; a *selector string* that will be sent to the gopher server to retrieve a document or a directory; the domain name of the host that has the document or directory; and a port number, which tells the gopher client and server how to connect over the TCP/IP connection.

0 ↳ About this gopher ↳ dog.mbu.edu ↳ 70

1 ↳ Places around town ↳ town. mbu.edu ↳ 70

1 ↳ Latest news ↳ news.mbu.edu ↳ 70

1 ↳ Other resources ↳ other.mbu.edu ↳ 70

8 ↳ Library of Congress ↳ locis.loc.gov ↳ 70

4 The gopher client displays only the user display string of each line. All these user display lines taken together is what makes up the gopher menu that you'll see.

Gopher

About this gopher
Places around town
Latest news
Other resources
Library of Congress

8 ↳ Library of Congress ↳ locis.loc.gov ↳ 70

5 When you choose an item from the gopher menu, the entire string—not just the string that you see—is sent from the client back to the gopher server. The number at the beginning of the string tells the server what kind of resource is being requested. A 0 means that the item is a file; a 1 means that the item is a directory; a 5 or a 9 means that the item is a binary file; a 7 means that a search will be launched; and an 8 points to a Telnet session.

Use Telnet on Library of Congress Info System

6 Using the selector string, the domain name, and the port number, in addition to the number at the beginning of the string, the server retrieves the information requested by the client. If the information requested was a directory, the gopher server will send a series of lines, each of which displays a menu option, just as was done when the server was first requested.

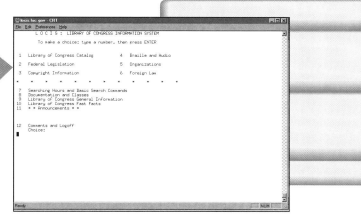

7 If the information requested was a search, the client software will be sent data allowing for a search.

8 If the information requested is a file or binary document, that file or document will be sent. Often, the information requested will be on a different server than the gopher server. In that event, the gopher server will contact the other server, and have the requested material sent to the gopher client. The gopher client can now read or otherwise use the material.

CHAPTER 15

How Telnet Works

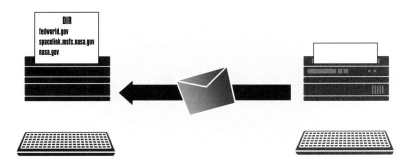

ONE of the more remarkable features of the Internet is the way it lets you use the resources of a distant computer somewhere else in the world. From your own home or office, you can log into another computer, issue commands just as if you were at that computer's keyboard, and then gain access to all of the computer's resources.

You do this with an Internet resource called Telnet. Telnet follows a client/server model, which means that you run a piece of software on your own PC—the client—to use the resources of a distant server computer. This distant computer is called the host. The host allows many different clients to access its resources at the same time; it isn't devoted to a single user. In order to use Telnet and the host's resources, you'll need to know the address of the Internet host whose resources you want to use.

When you use Telnet, before you can take over the resources of a host computer you'll typically have to log onto the host. Often, you can use the name "guest" to log in. Some systems require that you also give information about yourself, such as your name and address. And some may require that you choose a user name and a password that you will use the next time you log in.

There are many different hosts on the Internet that you can use Telnet to get access to. They are all different computers, so many of them don't work and look alike. As a way to make things easier, many hosts use a menuing system as a way to give you access to their resources. Also, when you connect using Telnet, you'll have to use *terminal emulation*—in essence you make sure that your keyboard and monitor function in the way that the host expects them to. The most common terminal emulation is the VT-100 emulation, so if you use Telnet software, that's a safe emulation to use.

There are Telnet clients available for all the major operating systems, including UNIX, Macintosh, and all versions of Windows. If you use an Internet shell account instead of a SLIP/PPP connection, you'll typically use a Telnet client by simply typing in the word **Telnet**, followed by the Internet address of the computer you want to access. For example, if you wanted to gain access to a computer run by the federal government called Fed World that lets you access a great deal of government information, you'd type in **Telnet fedworld.gov**. If you use a Telnet client for Windows or the Macintosh, Telnet is easier to use, since it will remember host names for you. With clients, you can often keep an address book of host names, so that you can easily revisit them.

How Telnet Works

Telnet allows you to use your computer to tap into the resources of a distant computer somewhere on the Internet. Among the many kinds of computers you can tap into using Telnet are libraries. From your own keyboard, you control the distant computer. You can see the results of what you do on your own computer screen. Telnet uses a client/server model, so that you need Telnet client software on your computer in order to use the resources of the distant computer, called a host.

1 In order to use Telnet, you need to know the Internet address of the host whose resources you want to use; your Telnet client contacts the host, using its Internet address.

2 When you contact the host, one of the first things that the distant computer and your computer does is negotiate how they will communicate with each other. They decide which *terminal emulation* will be used. Terminal emulation determines how your keyboard will transmit information to the distant computer, and how information will be displayed on your screen. It determines, for example, things such as how certain keys like the backspace key will work. The most common terminal emulation is referred to as VT-100.

Network Virtual Terminal

Network Virtual Terminal

3 When a client and a server communicate, they use the Telnet protocol. The Telnet protocol assumes that each end of the connection—the client and the server—is a Network Virtual Terminal (NVT). Each NVT has a virtual "printer" and a virtual "keyboard." The keyboard sends data from one NVT to the other. When you type in text on your keyboard, you're using the NVT keyboard. The printer is not really a printer at all—it receives and displays the data on the computer screen. When a distant Telnet connection sends you information and you display it on your screen, the printer is what is displaying it.

4 In a Telnet session, as you type text it accumulates in a buffer on your computer. When a complete line of data is ready for transmission, or when you give a command to transmit data (such as pressing the Enter key), the data is sent across the Internet from your NVT keyboard. Along with the data is the host's IP address, which makes sure that the packet is sent to the proper location.

5 Your IP address is also sent, so that information can be routed back to you. Additionally, specific Telnet commands are sent that the other NVT will use to decide what to do with the data, or how to respond to the data. For example, when data is sent from one NVT to another, and certain information must be sent back to the originating NVT in order for a process to proceed, the Telnet Go Ahead (GA) command is sent.

6 The Telnet host receives the data you've sent. It processes the data, and sends back to your screen—your NVT "printer"—the results of using the data or running the command on a distant computer. So, for example, if you type a series of keys with the letters dir and press Enter, the distant computer will carry out the dir command, and will send back to your screen the dir command and send the results of running that command on the distant computer.

7 Because packets have to go through many Internet routers in each direction between your computer and the host, there may be a delay between the time you send a command and when you see the results on your own computer screen.

CHAPTER

16

How WAIS Works

WAIS (wide area information server) provides a sophisticated way for you to find a vast array of information that resides on computers across the entire Internet. It lets you search databases without having to know any special search commands, and it gives you powerful ways to fine-tune your search so that you'll find more of the information that you want. With it, you'll be able to search a single database, or many databases simultaneously, and you'll be able to retrieve the information you want easily and store it on your own computer.

WAIS is what is known as a distributed system. In a *distributed system,* the data is spread among many computers, and is not only found on a single computer. The power of WAIS is that it lets you search on all the data distributed among many computers. It also allows for more sophisticated searching than standard Boolean systems.

The best way to use WAIS is to run client software on your own computer. Using that client software, you can search WAIS databases located on WAIS computers on the Internet. Your client software comes with a list of WAIS databases, and you can always add to that list as you come across new ones.

To begin a search, you type in a search request on your client software, and then using a special protocol, your client sends a request to a WAIS database. The database sends back a list of all the documents that match your search criteria. You can fine-tune your search, or pick the files you want transferred to your computer. Files can be data and text files, graphics, multimedia, or other files.

Every WAIS database is its own specialized library. Librarians at each site index the database into a kind of computerized card catalog so that it can be easily searched. WAIS sites frequently have FAQs or README files that give you more information on how to search that site.

You don't have to have a WAIS client on your own computer to search WAIS databases. You can use Telnet to access a public WAIS client that is located on a computer on the Internet. A gopher can also be used to search WAIS databases, but only one at a time.

WAIS client software gives you much more power than using Telnet or gopher. The client can save your searches so you can run them later, combine searches, rate the relevance of each document to your search, and much more. An especially powerful feature of WAIS client software is its ability to let you fine-tune your searches to a remarkable degree. If, for example, during your search you find a document that matches exactly the information you're looking for, you can tell your WAIS client to find other documents just like the one you've found. The WAIS client will then contact WAIS databases to seek out documents that closely match the documents you've already found. You'll then get a report telling you how relevant each of those new documents is to your search.

Searching with WAIS

A wide area information server, or WAIS, allows you to find vast amounts of information spread out across many databases on the Internet. It is a *distributed database,* which means that the data in it can be stored among many computers. WAIS databases are collections of information that cover a specific subject. There are hundreds of WAIS databases on the Internet covering many subjects. WAIS provides a comprehensive index of all the documents and files stored at WAIS databases. You can search through these indexes to quickly find the information you want.

1 You can search through a WAIS database using Telnet or gopher, but by far the best way to get the most out of the power of WAIS databases is by using a special WAIS client on your computer. WAIS clients will allow you to search many WAIS databases simultaneously, keep track of your searches and combine them, and help you narrow your search.

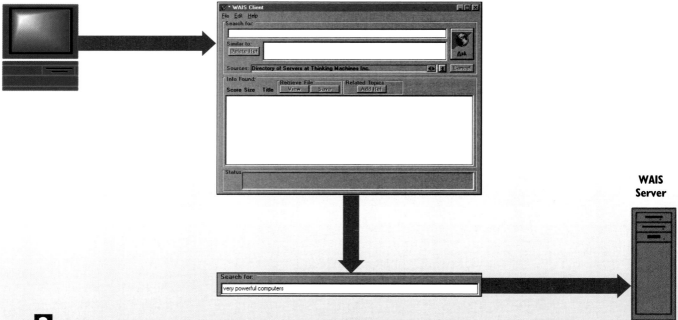

2 When you want to search a WAIS database, you compose a query on your WAIS client. Depending on your WAIS client, you can type in keywords to search for, or you can type in simple English statements or questions. You can send this search to a single WAIS database, or a group of them. You'll need to know the specific Internet locations of the WAIS databases in order to search through them. WAIS clients often come with a list of locations, and they provide ways for you to find more.

**WAIS
Server**

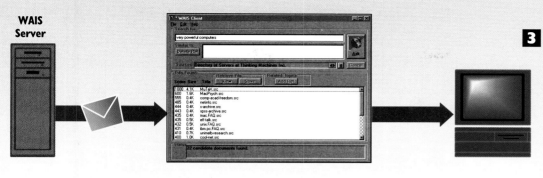

3 Your WAIS client translates your query into a special WAIS protocol, and then transmits the query over the Internet to a WAIS server. The server receives the request and translates the query into its own special query language. The server uses the query to search through the WAIS indexes, and finds documents that match what you're looking for.

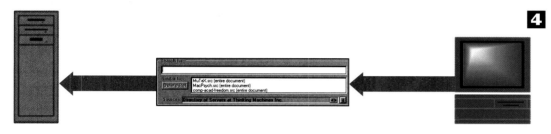

4 The server encodes the list of documents into the WAIS protocol and sends the results back to you. Your client software decodes the protocol, and displays the list of documents that match your search criteria. The documents are ranked in order of how relevant they are to your search, with the most relevant documents receiving the highest numerical ratings. You can now retrieve any of the documents in the list directly from the server.

5 One of WAIS's unique features is its ability to fine-tune searches. You can save your searches and run them at a later date to see if any new information is available. You can mark one or more of the list of documents sent to you as "relevant." You can then send a request to the WAIS server, asking that it send you a list of documents that most closely match the relevant one or ones you've marked.

Directory of WAIS Servers

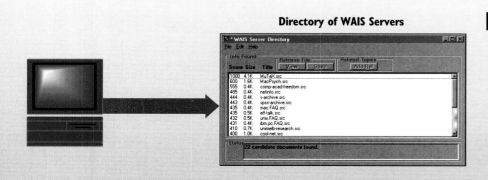

6 You can search a special WAIS database, called a directory of servers, to find out about new WAIS databases. After finding a new database that interests you, you can add the WAIS database's Internet address to your computer. This is like looking up a phone number for a new business in the yellow pages, then adding the number to your own speed dialer.

C H A P T E R

17

FTP and Downloading Files

ONE of the most popular uses of the Internet is to download files—that is, transfer files from a computer on the Internet to your computer. These files can be of many types: programs that you can run on your own computer; graphics you can view; sounds and music you can listen to; or text files that you can read. Many tens of thousands of files are downloaded every day on the Internet. Most of those files are downloaded using the Internet's *File Transfer Protocol*, commonly referred to as FTP. FTP can also be used to upload files from your computer to another computer on the Internet.

FTP, like many Internet resources, works on a client/server model. You run FTP client software on your computer to connect to an FTP server on the Internet. On the FTP server, a program called an *FTP daemon* allows you to download and upload files.

In order to log onto an FTP site and download files, an account number (or user name) and a password must be typed in before the daemon will allow you to enter. Some sites allow anyone to enter and download files—but an account number (or user name) and password must be entered. Often, to get in you use "anonymous" as your user name and your e-mail address as your password. Because of this, these sites are often referred to as *anonymous FTP* sites. Some FTP sites are private, only allowing certain people with the proper account number and password to enter.

FTP is fairly simple to use. When you log onto an FTP site, you can browse through the available files by changing directories, and you can see a listing of all the files available in each directory. When you see a file you want to download, you use your client software to instruct the FTP server to send you the file.

As the World Wide Web gains popularity, downloading software is becoming even easier. You can use your Web browser, and click on links to files. In fact, though, behind the scenes FTP is still downloading the files. FTP is still the most popular way to download files from the Web and the Internet.

One problem with downloading files over the Internet is that some files are so large that it can take a tremendous amount of time to download them, especially if the connection is made via modem. Even at 28,800 bps, downloading files can be slow. As a way to speed up file transfers, files are commonly compressed—shrunk in size using special compression software. After the files have been downloaded, you'll need to run the compression software on your own computer to decompress the files so that you can use them.

How an FTP Session Works

A common way to transfer files from the Internet to your computer is to use FTP, or File Transfer Protocol. FTP can also be used to upload a file to a computer on the Internet, although this is a less frequent use of FTP. Even when you download files to your computer using a World Wide Web browser, you often use FTP, although you won't necessarily know that.

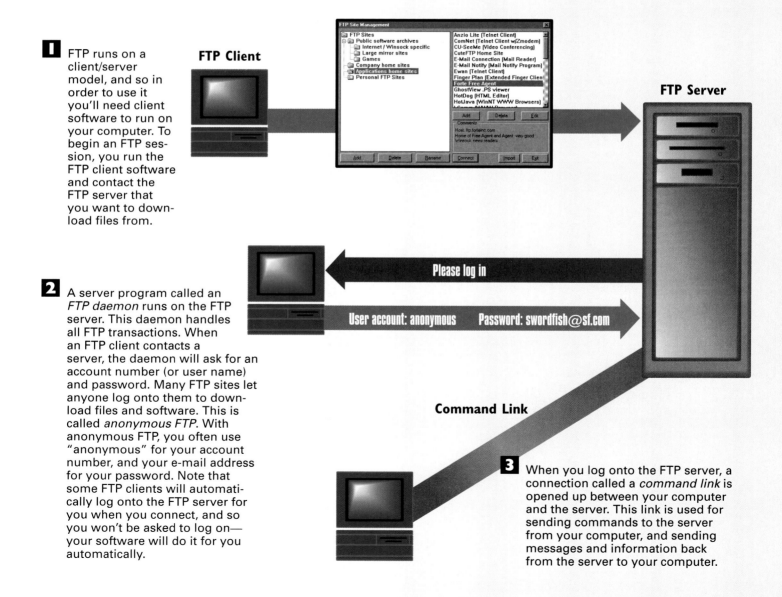

1 FTP runs on a client/server model, and so in order to use it you'll need client software to run on your computer. To begin an FTP session, you run the FTP client software and contact the FTP server that you want to download files from.

FTP Client

FTP Server

Please log in

User account: anonymous   Password: swordfish@sf.com

Command Link

2 A server program called an *FTP daemon* runs on the FTP server. This daemon handles all FTP transactions. When an FTP client contacts a server, the daemon will ask for an account number (or user name) and password. Many FTP sites let anyone log onto them to download files and software. This is called *anonymous FTP*. With anonymous FTP, you often use "anonymous" for your account number, and your e-mail address for your password. Note that some FTP clients will automatically log onto the FTP server for you when you connect, and so you won't be asked to log on—your software will do it for you automatically.

3 When you log onto the FTP server, a connection called a *command link* is opened up between your computer and the server. This link is used for sending commands to the server from your computer, and sending messages and information back from the server to your computer.

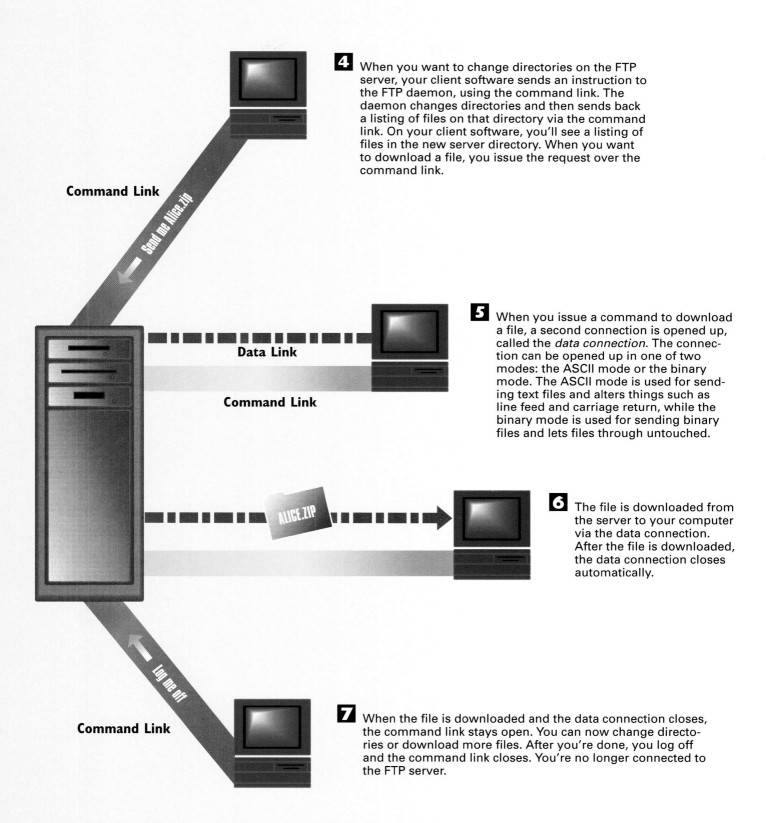

4 When you want to change directories on the FTP server, your client software sends an instruction to the FTP daemon, using the command link. The daemon changes directories and then sends back a listing of files on that directory via the command link. On your client software, you'll see a listing of files in the new server directory. When you want to download a file, you issue the request over the command link.

Command Link

Send me Alice.zip

Data Link

Command Link

5 When you issue a command to download a file, a second connection is opened up, called the *data connection*. The connection can be opened up in one of two modes: the ASCII mode or the binary mode. The ASCII mode is used for sending text files and alters things such as line feed and carriage return, while the binary mode is used for sending binary files and lets files through untouched.

ALICE.ZIP

6 The file is downloaded from the server to your computer via the data connection. After the file is downloaded, the data connection closes automatically.

Log me off

Command Link

7 When the file is downloaded and the data connection closes, the command link stays open. You can now change directories or download more files. After you're done, you log off and the command link closes. You're no longer connected to the FTP server.

How File Compression Works

Many files on the Internet are compressed to save space on the FTP server, and to save time when they traveling across the Internet. Many different methods are used to compress files. Depending on the file type, files are usually compressed from 10 to 50 percent.

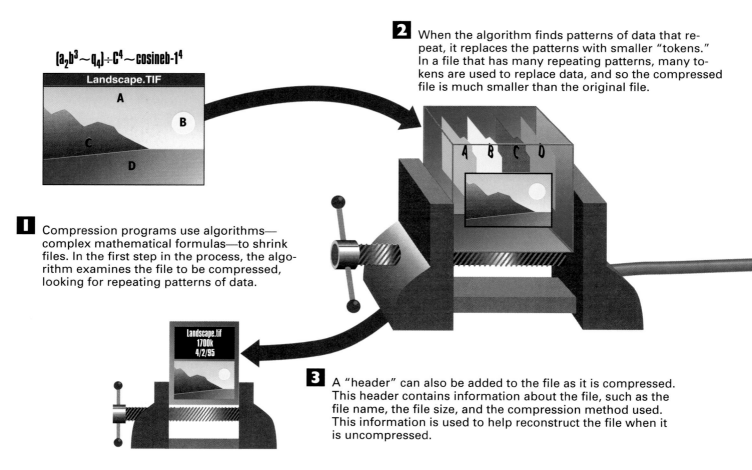

$$(a_2b^3 \sim q_4) \div C^4 \sim cosineb\text{-}1^4$$

2 When the algorithm finds patterns of data that repeat, it replaces the patterns with smaller "tokens." In a file that has many repeating patterns, many tokens are used to replace data, and so the compressed file is much smaller than the original file.

1 Compression programs use algorithms—complex mathematical formulas—to shrink files. In the first step in the process, the algorithm examines the file to be compressed, looking for repeating patterns of data.

3 A "header" can also be added to the file as it is compressed. This header contains information about the file, such as the file name, the file size, and the compression method used. This information is used to help reconstruct the file when it is uncompressed.

Types of File-Compression Schemes You'll Find on the Internet

File extensions, the letters that appear after the period at the end of a file name, can tell you if and how a file is compressed.

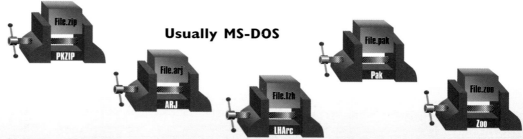

Usually MS-DOS

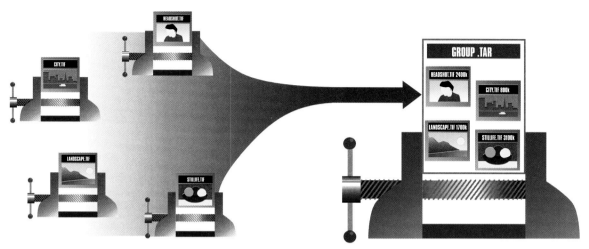

4 Some compression software, such as PKZIP for the PC, can also *archive* files—combining several compressed files. The UNIX command TAR can also combine many files into a single archive.

5 When you want to use a compressed file you find on the Internet, you transfer it over the Internet to your computer.

$(a_2b^3 \sim q_4) \div C^4 \sim cosineb\text{-}1^4$

6 In order to use the file, you'll need decompression software on your computer. The decompression software looks into the file's header, and examines the tokens in the file. Using a decompression algorithm, it reconstructs the original file, which you can then use on your computer.

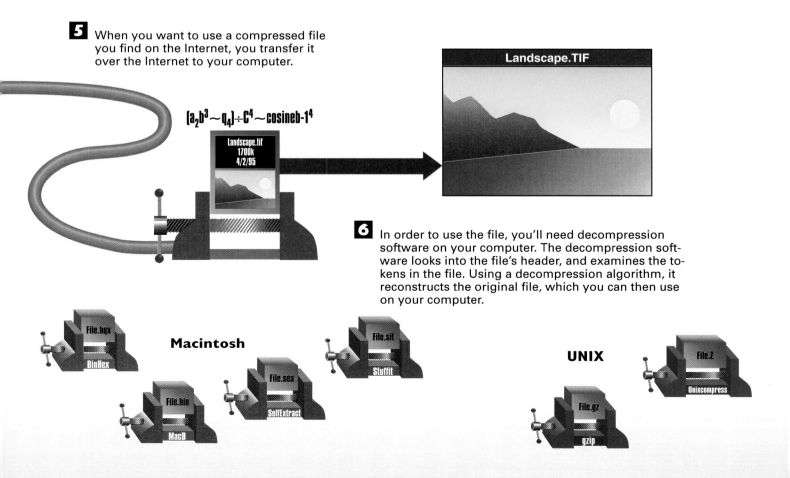

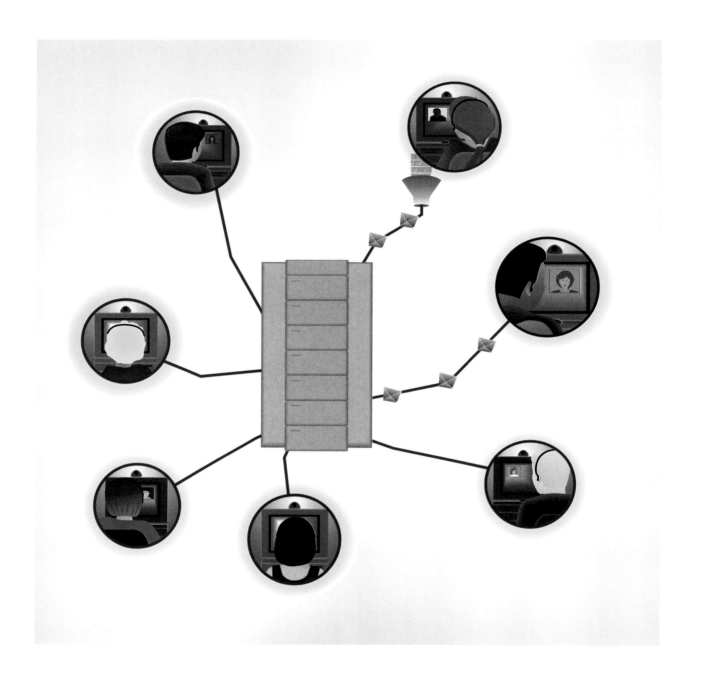

P A R T

MULTIMEDIA ON THE INTERNET

POSSIBLY

the most dramatic and remarkable part of the Internet is the multimedia content you'll find on it. You'll be able to listen to music, sound clips, and live radio stations from your computer. You can watch astronauts live while they're on the space shuttle. You can watch video clips of the news and other events. And you can even have live video conferencing with people from all over the world.

You can do all that with the Internet's audio and video capabilities. You won't need specialized hardware and software to do it—and in many cases, you won't even need a very high-speed Internet connection. An ordinary dial-in connection to the Internet will do, although the sound and video quality will be better at high speeds. And you'll only need free or inexpensive software, and a sound card and speakers that ship with most computers, or that are available separately.

The Internet's multimedia capabilities go beyond the playing of audio and video clips. You can participate in virtual worlds, and join in "virtual chat" sessions in which you build your own online persona called an "avatar" and communicate and interact with other avatars. The Internet allows for the creation of remarkable online multimedia content, combining animation, sound, and programming, via technologies such as the Java programming language.

In this section of the book, we'll look at how every aspect of multimedia on the Internet works. Chapter 18 covers audio on the Internet. We'll see how audio files are sent to your computer and played. And we'll look in detail at how *streaming audio* works. Streaming audio allows you to play sounds and music on your computer while the audio file is being transferred to your computer, so that you don't have to wait for the file to download.

Chapter 19 details how video works on the Internet. We'll first see how the MBone works—a high-speed Internet backbone that is used for transmitting video across the Internet. And we'll look at how streaming video works, which—like streaming audio—lets you watch a video while it is being downloaded to your computer. And we'll also look at how the Internet allows you to do video conferencing—to see and talk to others using your computer.

Chapter 20 turns to a lighter topic: how NetCams work. NetCams are cameras on the Internet that at regular intervals broadcast a photograph or animation. There are NetCams all over the world, from the top of Pike's Peak to the streets of Hong Kong.

Finally, Chapters 21 and 22 take a look at virtual reality and multimedia programming. We'll look at some of the most exciting technology on the Internet today. We'll look at how virtual reality works, and at several ways that you can view multimedia programming on the Internet with technologies such as Java and Shockwave.

CHAPTER

18

Audio on the Internet

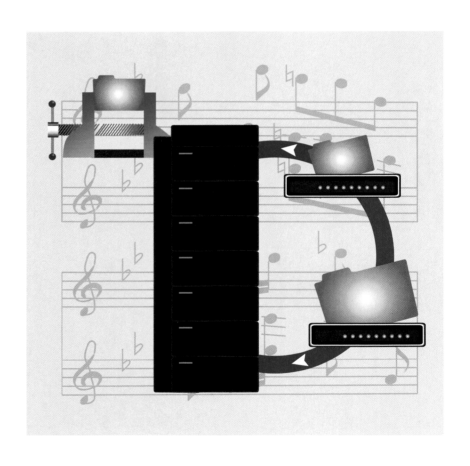

SOUNDS,

voices, and music are now an everyday part of the Internet. Through the Internet, you can listen to radio stations, interviews, music, sound clips, and much more.

One of the most intriguing experimental uses of audio on the Internet is Internet Talk Radio. Modeled after National Public Radio, it features special affairs programs, interviews, and a variety of special reports. Probably the best-known show on Internet Talk Radio is "Geek of the Week," in which an Internet expert was interviewed every week.

While Internet Talk Radio has been popular, it has also been hampered by a technology limitation. In order to listen to it on your computer, you have to download audio files to your computer. Once they are on your computer, you can listen to them using special audio software and a sound card. The problem is that the files are very large—often well over 10 megabytes—so it can take hours to get them transferred to your computer before you can listen to them.

There are many other kinds of audio files you'll be able to find on the Internet. They all have one thing in common: They have been digitized so that a computer can play them. You'll find many music files and sound clips in a variety of sound formats. Each of those formats has a different extension associated with them, such as .WAV or .AU. In order to play those files, you'll first have to download them, and then have audio player software play them on your computer. Netscape and other browsers have some of these software players built in. For other formats, you'll have to find and download the player, and then configure your browser properly in order to play them.

Most sound files tend to be quite large, even after being compressed. You won't be able to listen to them until the entire file is downloaded, which can take quite a while. It may take you 15 minutes to download a sound file that has less than a minute of sound in it.

A far better—and newer—use of audio on the Internet is called *streaming audio*. It handles audio in a much more clever way. With streaming audio, you don't have to wait until the entire audio file is downloaded in order to play it. Instead, you listen to the audio while it downloads to your computer. There are a variety of technologies that allow for streaming audio. For all of them, you'll need to have the proper audio player, and you'll need a different audio player for each different kind of streaming audio. In this chapter we'll look at one of the most popular audio streaming technologies, called RealAudio.

How RealAudio Streaming Audio Works

There are a number of different ways to play streaming audio (audio that plays in real time), as it gets sent to your computer. A very popular one is called RealAudio. In order to play RealAudio clips, you need a RealAudio software player on your computer. Some World Wide Web browsers have the RealAudio player built in. If yours doesn't, you can download the player and configure it to work with your browser.

■ When you use your Web browser and click on a link to a RealAudio sound clip on a home page, the link doesn't lead directly to a sound file. Instead, your Web browser contacts the Web server, which sends back to your browser a file called a RealAudio *metafile*. This metafile is a small text file that has the true location—the URL—of the RealAudio sound file you want to play, and also has instructions that tell your Web browser to launch the RealAudio sound player, which is required in order to play the clip.

Launch RealAudio Player
Contact
http://www.sound.com/music.ra

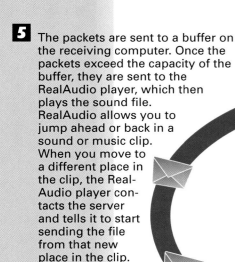

5 The packets are sent to a buffer on the receiving computer. Once the packets exceed the capacity of the buffer, they are sent to the RealAudio player, which then plays the sound file. RealAudio allows you to jump ahead or back in a sound or music clip. When you move to a different place in the clip, the Real-Audio player contacts the server and tells it to start sending the file from that new place in the clip.

4 The RealAudio clip has been compressed and encoded. If the file wasn't compressed, the sound file would be too large and so would take too long to send and be played. The clip is sent in IP packets using the UDP (User Datagram Protocol) instead of the Internet's normal TCP (Transmission Control Protocol). UDP doesn't keep resending packets if they are misplaced or other problems occur, as does TCP. If packets had to keep being re-sent, the sound player on the receiving end could be constantly interrupted with packets, and so could not play the clip.

3 The RealAudio server and the RealAudio sound player "talk" to one another so that the server knows at what speed the user is connected to the Internet. If the connection is a low-speed connection, a smaller RealAudio file is sent that contains less data. This will be a file of lesser quality than a file sent via a high-speed connection. If a high-speed connection is used, a larger, higher-quality sound file is sent. This will provide for better sound quality.

Get http://www.sound.com/music.ra

2 The metafile launches the Real-Audio sound player, which contacts the URL contained in the metafile. The URL it contacts is not on the Web server. Instead, it is on a different RealAudio server designed to deliver RealAudio sound clips.

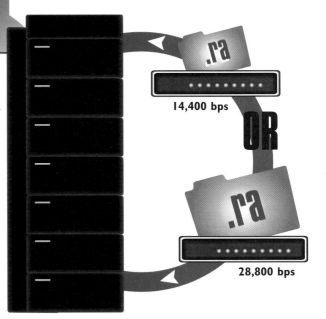

RealAudio Server

14,400 bps

28,800 bps

OR

CHAPTER

19

Video on the Internet

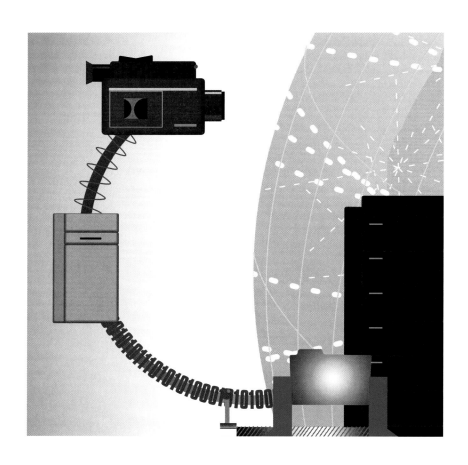

THE Internet began as a way for people to share text-based information: electronic mail, discussion groups, and file transfers. Today, though, the technology has advanced far beyond text. Today on the Internet you can have video conferences in which you talk live with someone and see them live on your computer screen. You can have "white board" applications in which you see and talk to each other, and also work on a file together live on your computer screens. You can watch live video footage of astronauts from outer space. And you can watch taped videos from a number of different sources, whenever you want—not when a national broadcaster says you must watch them.

To understand how all this works, you'll need to understand three kinds of technologies. The first is called the *MBone* (*Multicast Backbone*), a special Internet high-speed backbone capable of sending vast amounts of information. Many video transmissions—especially live ones—are sent across the MBone because of its high bandwidth.

The second technology is called *streaming video*. Streaming video solves a long-standing problem of sending video signals across the Internet. Video files tend to be extremely large because they have so much information packed into them. Because of that, sending video was never very practical—it could take hours to send a single video file to someone's computer. They would have to wait until the entire file was downloaded, and then play it—and it might play for only a few minutes.

Streaming video solves the problem in two ways. First, it compresses the video file dramatically, so it is much smaller as it's transmitted across the Internet. And secondly, it lets the receiving computer start playing the video while the file is being transmitted. So if you receive a streaming video file, you watch the video as you receive it; no waiting for the entire file to download. Streaming video files are not usually live broadcasts. Instead, they are files that are created ahead of time, and then posted on the Internet. Whenever you want, you can watch the video just by clicking on its hypertext link. You'll need a special player in order to watch the video. There are a number of different ways to send streaming video across the Internet. In this chapter we'll look at one of the most popular, called VDOLive.

The third piece of technology is video conferencing. It lets you have live video conferences across the Internet using your computer. Video conferencing is done live, although the technology can also be used to broadcast taped videos as well. NASA, the National Aeronautics and Space Administration, sometimes uses the technology to broadcast live from the Space Shuttle, and also to broadcast taped videos about space exploration. In this chapter we'll look at the oldest and most popular means of video conferencing—CU-SeeMe.

How the MBone Works

1 The MBone (Multicast Backbone) is a high-speed Internet connection capable of sending live video and audio transmissions. MBone is a network of host computers that communicate with each other using a technique called IP (Internet Protocol) multicast. An MBone multicast begins when a video signal is digitized and compressed so that it can be sent out over the Internet. Without compression the signal would be too large and take too long to deliver.

010100010010101010101000101000111110101001

2 The compressed, digitized signal is sent in packets using IP multicast protocol, instead of the Internet's normal TCP. The multicast protocol allows the signal to be sent to a number of sites on the Internet simultaneously. Normally, the Internet is unicast, which means that each signal can be sent only to a single specific destination.

IP

IP Multicast Protocol

IP Multicast Protocol

3 A major advantage of the multicast protocol is that when the video packets are sent—for example from Europe to the United States—they are sent only one time, even though they may be sent to many destinations. Normally, TCP would have to send separate video packets for each destination. The multicast protocol solves the problem by putting information about the many Internet destinations within the packet itself, so that later on in the transmission the video signals will be delivered to each of the destinations.

MBone

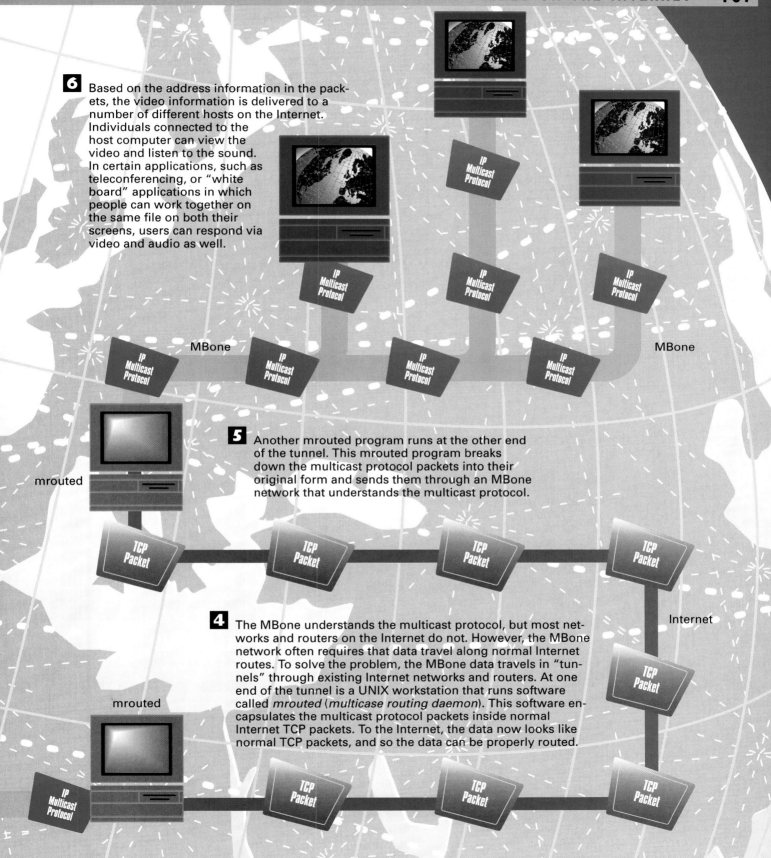

6 Based on the address information in the packets, the video information is delivered to a number of different hosts on the Internet. Individuals connected to the host computer can view the video and listen to the sound. In certain applications, such as teleconferencing, or "white board" applications in which people can work together on the same file on both their screens, users can respond via video and audio as well.

MBone

MBone

mrouted

5 Another mrouted program runs at the other end of the tunnel. This mrouted program breaks down the multicast protocol packets into their original form and sends them through an MBone network that understands the multicast protocol.

Internet

mrouted

4 The MBone understands the multicast protocol, but most networks and routers on the Internet do not. However, the MBone network often requires that data travel along normal Internet routes. To solve the problem, the MBone data travels in "tunnels" through existing Internet networks and routers. At one end of the tunnel is a UNIX workstation that runs software called *mrouted (multicase routing daemon)*. This software encapsulates the multicast protocol packets inside normal Internet TCP packets. To the Internet, the data now looks like normal TCP packets, and so the data can be properly routed.

How Streaming Video Works

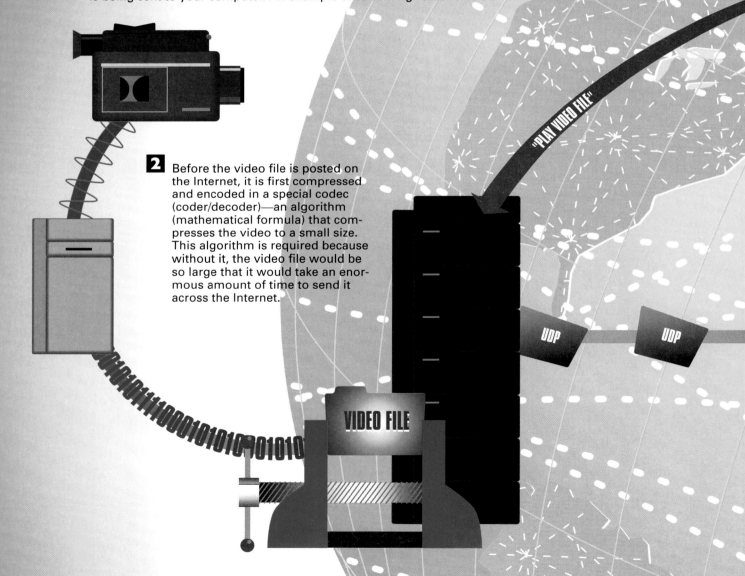

1 Streaming video refers to video that you can play live on the Internet—you don't have to wait until the download is complete to see the video. Instead, you can play the video while it is being sent to your computer. An example of streaming video is VDOLive.

2 Before the video file is posted on the Internet, it is first compressed and encoded in a special codec (coder/decoder)—an algorithm (mathematical formula) that compresses the video to a small size. This algorithm is required because without it, the video file would be so large that it would take an enormous amount of time to send it across the Internet.

"PLAY VIDEO FILE"

VIDEO FILE

UDP

UDP

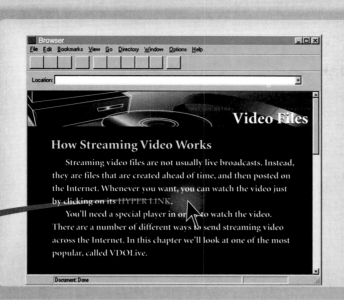

3 When you send a request to see the video by clicking on an icon or a link on a World Wide Web page, you are sending a message from your computer to a server asking for the video file. The server sends the file to you across the Internet. It sends the file in packets, using the IP protocol. It does not use the normal Internet TCP, though. Instead it uses the UDP (User Datagram Protocol). Unlike TCP, the UDP does not constantly check to see if data has been sent, and so it results in a more uninterrupted file transfer.

4 The video packets are sent to a buffer in your computer—an area of memory that ranges between 5K and 30K. The server can tell by how fast the buffer fills up what speed connection you have to the server. At higher speeds it will send more video data, and you will get a smoother, more life-like video. At lower speeds, it sends less data and so the video quality suffers.

5 When the buffer fills up, which takes only a few seconds, a video player is launched on your computer. You can now watch the video on the player. As you watch the video, video packets are still being delivered to your buffer. Data from the buffer is continually sent to the player so that you can watch an entire video. When all the video data has been sent, the video will stop. The video file does not stay on your system; each section of the file is discarded after it is played.

How CU-SeeMe Video Conferencing Works

1 There are a variety of ways for people to video conference across the Internet. One of the first and the most popular is CU-SeeMe. CU-SeeMe allows people with desktop computers to have live video conferences with individuals and groups anywhere on the Internet. Using inexpensive software and hardware, anyone can do video conferencing.

2 When one person wants to video conference with someone else, he or she uses CU-SeMee software to log into a *reflector*. A reflector is an Internet computer that hosts many live video conferences that people can join. When you log into a reflector, you can join any conference that exists. When someone is logged into a reflector, a signal goes out regularly from the person's computer to the reflector, telling everyone connected to the reflector that the person is logged in and available for a video conference.

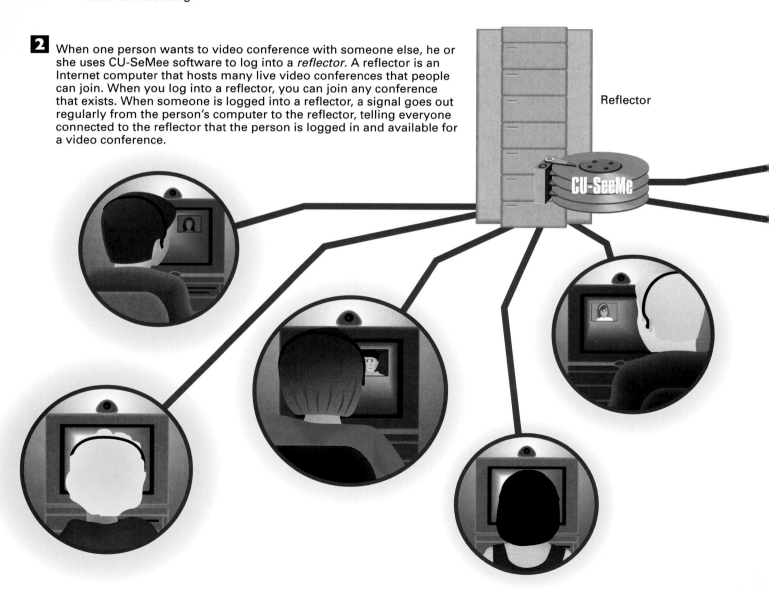

Reflector

CU-SeeMe

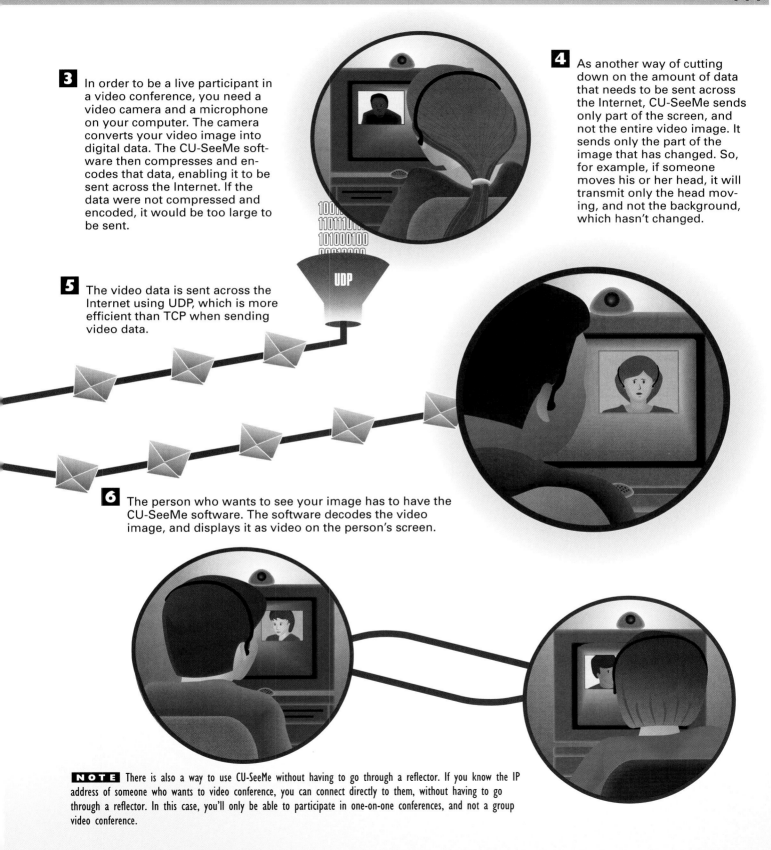

3 In order to be a live participant in a video conference, you need a video camera and a microphone on your computer. The camera converts your video image into digital data. The CU-SeeMe software then compresses and encodes that data, enabling it to be sent across the Internet. If the data were not compressed and encoded, it would be too large to be sent.

4 As another way of cutting down on the amount of data that needs to be sent across the Internet, CU-SeeMe sends only part of the screen, and not the entire video image. It sends only the part of the image that has changed. So, for example, if someone moves his or her head, it will transmit only the head moving, and not the background, which hasn't changed.

UDP

5 The video data is sent across the Internet using UDP, which is more efficient than TCP when sending video data.

6 The person who wants to see your image has to have the CU-SeeMe software. The software decodes the video image, and displays it as video on the person's screen.

NOTE There is also a way to use CU-SeeMe without having to go through a reflector. If you know the IP address of someone who wants to video conference, you can connect directly to them, without having to go through a reflector. In this case, you'll only be able to participate in one-on-one conferences, and not a group video conference.

CHAPTER
20

How NetCams Work

PART of the joy of using the Internet is the sheer pleasure that you can get in finding something that is amazing, albeit not particularly useful. Call it the "coolness" factor, but for whatever reasons, many people enjoy surfing the Internet just to find intriguing bits of information and technology. NetCams assist in that endeavor. A NetCam is a camera attached to the Internet that automatically takes photographs at certain intervals, and then broadcasts those photographs to the world. There are NetCams focused on a variety of subjects. You can see the weather on top of Pike's Peak, view the Boston skyline from the banks of Cambridge's Charles River, see a Hong Kong street scene, view a golf course on Maui, watch tropical fish swim lazily in an aquarium or a parrot hop around its cage—just for starters. There's something intriguing and remarkable about being able to see live scenes from anywhere in the world while you're sitting at your own computer.

The way NetCams work is actually quite simple. A video camera sends an image to a computer, which then converts the image into a binary format that computers can read. It then posts the image on the Internet for anyone to see.

While today NetCams are primarily used for sheer fun, they may eventually serve many useful purposes. They could conceivably be used to monitor and reroute traffic to prevent rush hour gridlock. They could be used as security cameras. No doubt, there will be many other uses for NetCams as well.

NetCams are only one in a sometimes-bizarre genre of Internet resources—devices of various sorts that are hooked up to the Internet. One of the first and most famous was a soda machine. Anyone from anywhere in the world could check to see what soda was available from the machine. There are now many soda machines (and cappuccino makers) across the world; you can check if you'd like. There are also CD players you can check to see what song is playing—and even change the track on the CD from your own keyboard, as well as listen to snippets of what is playing.

More intriguing—and potentially useful in the long run—are the robots you can control from your keyboard. There are a growing number of these. In one, you can help excavate an archaeological site by blowing sand away from an area, digging and then viewing, through a video camera, to see what you've done. You can also remotely control a telescope. And you can control a mobile robot from your keyboard, navigating it through a building from your own computer.

How NetCams Work

A NetCam is a camera hooked up to the Internet that automatically broadcasts photographs or moving images so that anyone on the Internet can see them. There are hundreds of NetCams on the Internet, sending live pictures from all over the world.

4 When someone clicks on the link, the picture is sent to his or her Web browser and displayed. Some NetCams appear to send live video images, so that the NetCam image on your computer isn't a photograph, but instead appears to be a moving image. In fact, the "moving image" is a series of photographs sent every few seconds that give the illusion of movement. When you click on the link to the image, the images will automatically be sent to your Web browser as they are updated by the video camera.

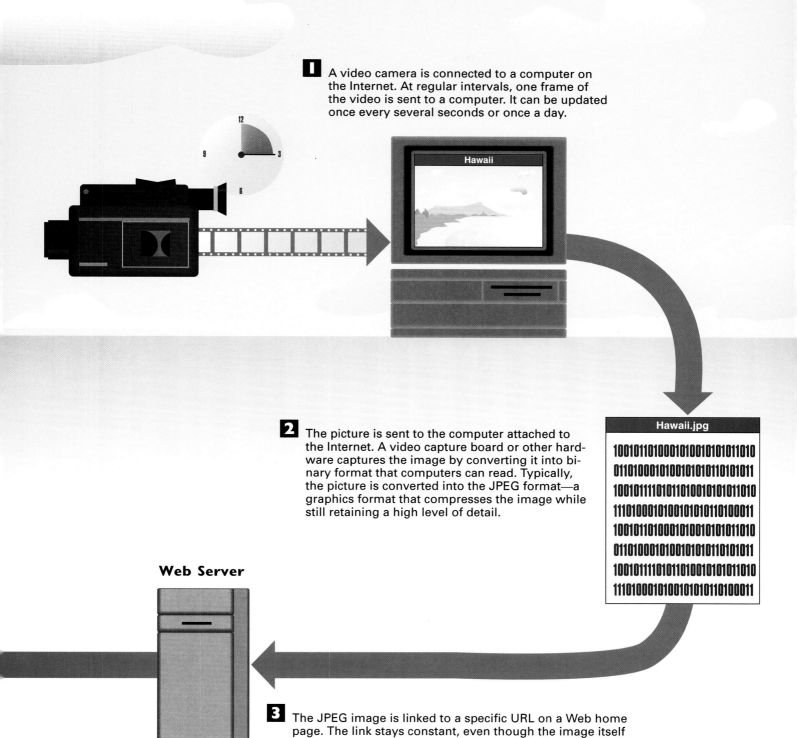

1 A video camera is connected to a computer on the Internet. At regular intervals, one frame of the video is sent to a computer. It can be updated once every several seconds or once a day.

Hawaii

Hawaii.jpg

2 The picture is sent to the computer attached to the Internet. A video capture board or other hardware captures the image by converting it into binary format that computers can read. Typically, the picture is converted into the JPEG format—a graphics format that compresses the image while still retaining a high level of detail.

Web Server

3 The JPEG image is linked to a specific URL on a Web home page. The link stays constant, even though the image itself changes regularly. That means that whenever someone clicks on the link, they will see the most recent picture that was taken by the NetCam.

C H A P T E R
21

Virtual Reality on the Internet

IMAGINE

the Internet as a place where you were able to walk through three-dimensional worlds, pick up objects, examine them, and go to other Internet locations by flying or walking through doors. Picture home pages that were more than flat, two-dimensional surfaces that you could only read. What if you could be inside them, just like you can walk through a city or a building?

That's the promise of virtual reality (VR) on the Internet. In fact, it's more than just a promise—virtual reality is already here. You'll find many virtual worlds you can explore on the Internet. You'll be able to walk through a giant computer, explore bizarre art galleries, visit outer space, go to the sites of what seem like ancient ruins, explore inside the human brain, and much more.

Virtual worlds are created using a computer language called *Virtual Reality Modeling Language (VRML)*. This language instructs computers on how to build three-dimensional geometric objects. Programmers and artists use the language to build complex worlds from these geometric objects. A VRML world is created by an ASCII text file containing VRML language commands—and for greater realism, graphics files can be added to this world as well. Because the virtual world is only an ASCII file, with perhaps a few graphics files, it can be downloaded quickly to your computer from the Internet.

When a virtual world is created, it is posted on an Internet server. When you want to visit that world, you either type in its URL or click on a link to it, just as you do to visit any other location on the World Wide Web. To display the virtual world, you'll need to have a program able to display the world—either a separate virtual reality browser, or more likely, a plug-in player that configures itself to your normal Web browser.

The VRML file describing the virtual world downloads to your computer. This can take a few minutes, or well over half an hour, depending on the size of the world and your connection speed. Once the file is on your computer, your CPU computes the geometry of the world, based on the VRML commands in the file. Again, depending on the size of the world and the speed of your CPU, this can take only a minute or two, or up to ten minutes or more. Once the world is computed, you can walk through it, fly through it, examine objects, and spin them. You can also visit other virtual worlds or places on the Internet by interacting with the world.

Virtual reality on the Internet is being used for far more than just creating virtual worlds that people can walk through. For example, it has been used to create views of the brain and of molecules. It has been used by astronomers to show the rotation of molecular gas in a galaxy undergoing active star formation. And as with everything else having to do with the Internet, it will be used for things that today none of us can imagine.

How Virtual Reality Works

Virtual Reality (VR) locations—also called virtual worlds—on the Internet let you walk through and interact with three-dimensional worlds using a special plug-in program connected to your Web browser. These locations are built using the Virtual Reality Modeling Language (VRML). In order to enter virtual worlds, you'll need either a virtual reality Web browser or a plug-in program that installs inside your Web browser and lets you visit virtual worlds. Plug-ins are more popular than separate programs.

1 When someone wants to create a virtual world, he or she uses the VRML language. The language lets people create three-dimensional worlds not by drawing them, but instead by using the VRML computer language to describe the geometry of a scene. VRML files are much smaller than graphics files. VRML files are simply text files that contain instructions for drawing the VRML world. VRML files end in a .WRL extension. After the world is created, it is posted on a Web server.

```
======== SPACE.WRL ========
#VRML V1.Ø ascii
Separator {
    DirectionalLight {
        direction Ø Ø -1  # Light shining from
viewer into scene
    PerspectiveCamera {
        position    -8.6 2.1 5.6
        orientation -Ø.1352 -Ø.9831 -Ø.1233
1.1417
        focalDistance       1Ø.84
    }
```

SPACE.WRL

```
========== OBJECTS.WRL ==========
#VRML V1.Ø ascii
Separator {
    DirectionalLight {
        direction Ø Ø -1  # Light shining from viewer into scene
    }
    PerspectiveCamera {
        position    -8.6 2.1 5.6
        orientation -Ø.1352 -Ø.9831 -Ø.1233  1.1417
        focalDistance       1Ø.84
    }
    Separator {   # The red sphere
        Material {
            diffuseColor 1 Ø Ø   # Red
        }
        Translation { translation 3 Ø 1 }
        Sphere { radius 2.3 }
    }
    Separator {   # The blue cube
        Material {
            diffuseColor Ø Ø 1  # Blue
        }
        Transform {
            translation -2.4 .2 1
            rotation Ø 1 1  .9
        }
        Cube {}
    }
}
```

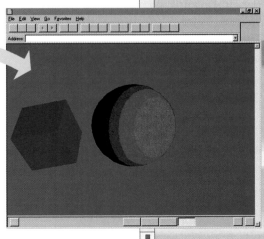

2 Here is an example of a VRML file describing a scene that has a red sphere and a blue cube in it, lit by a directional light.

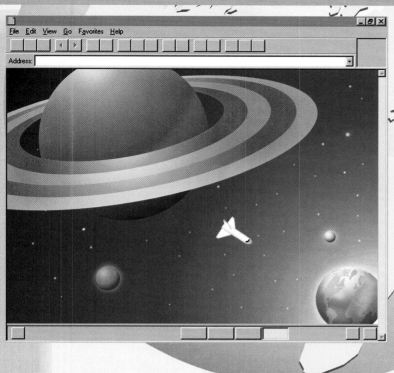

6 For greater realism and detail, graphics files can be "painted" on virtual reality objects, for example, to show paintings in an art gallery. When these graphics files are painted on objects, they must be downloaded along with the .WRL file as GIF or JPEG files. When the browser displays the virtual world, it shows those graphics files on top of VR objects so that they look like part of the scene.

5 Objects in the virtual world can be links to sites on the Web, to other virtual worlds, and to animations. So, for example, if you walk through a door, you might be sent to a home page on the Internet, or to another virtual world. If you're sent to another virtual world, that virtual world will have to be downloaded from a Web server to your computer so that your browser can compute the new world and you can interact with it.

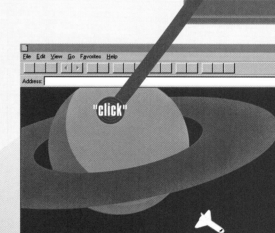

4 As the file downloads, the VR plug-in is launched. It doesn't run separately from your Web browser. Instead, it takes over your Web browser while you're in the virtual world. After the file is downloaded, your VR plug-in creates the virtual world by taking the VRML commands in the file and having your computer compute the geometry of the scene. Once the computation is done, the scene will appear on your screen. The VRML file contains three-dimensional information so that you can walk or fly through the scene using your browser. Depending upon the complexity of the scene, your computer may have to do computations as you move through the scene.

Web Server

3 When you have a VR plug-in installed on your Web browser you can visit a virtual world by clicking on its URL. The first thing that happens is that the VRML file is sent from the Web server to your computer. Depending on the size of the virtual world and your connection speed, the file can take from a few minutes to a half-hour or more to download to your computer.

CHAPTER

22

Multimedia Programming on the Internet

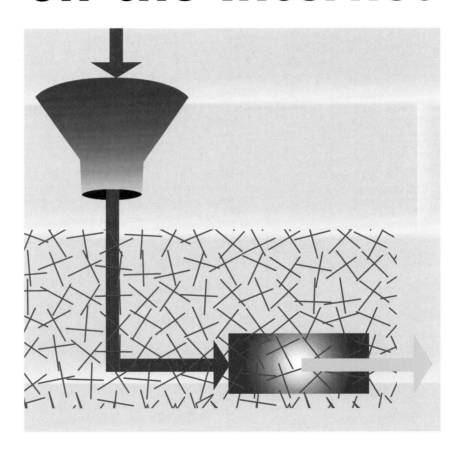

THE Internet of tomorrow will be very different from the Internet we see today. Most people believe that the greatest change will involve interactivity and multimedia. Home pages will not be flat documents to be merely read or looked at—instead they will have animation, music, and sound; they will present information in remarkable new ways and allow for interaction between you and the Internet.

That's already begun to happen in a big way. A generation of languages and tools has been created that allows interactive programming to be developed for the World Wide Web. This allows for all kinds of things never before possible on the Internet: news tickers that flash breaking news across home pages; interactive games of all sorts; and multimedia presentations combining animation, sound, music, and graphics much like sophisticated television shows or computer CD-ROMs.

A variety of these tools are transforming the Internet, and most particularly the World Wide Web. Shockwave, for example, is a plug-in to a Web browser that lets you view multimedia presentations created by the powerful multimedia authoring program Director from Macromedia. When you install Shockwave as a plug-in, whenever you visit a Web page that has Shockwave files those files will download to your computer, where they will be played by your plug-in.

Even more important, and what many people believe will likely have most to do with the transformation of the Web, is a computer language developed by Sun Microsystems called Java. Java allows for more sophisticated programming than Shockwave does. While Shockwave is a multimedia presentation, Java programs are true applications, just like the word processing and spreadsheet programs you run on your computer.

Java programs run inside your Web browser, if you have what is called a "Java-enabled" browser such as Netscape. When Java programs are run inside a browser, they are called applets. If you have a Java-enabled browser, you don't need to do anything to run a Java applet. When you visit a Web site that has a Java applet on it, the applet is downloaded to your computer from a Web server. Once the applet is on your computer, it will run automatically. Today, common Java applets are news tickers that run across Web pages, and animations.

Java and Shockwave are only two of the kinds of languages and tools that allow for interactive programming on the Internet. Many people believe that these kinds of programs in general—and Java in particular—will become so popular that they will transform not just the Internet, but computing in general. They believe that low-cost computers called "Internet appliances" that could sell for $500 will be as powerful as computers costing many times that because hard disks and a lot of local processing power won't be necessary if Java applets and other Internet interactive programs are able to run on them.

Whether or not that becomes a reality, multimedia programming has already changed the face of the Internet—and will continue to in the future.

How Java Works

Java is a programming language developed by Sun Microsystems that allows programmers, editors, and artists to create interactive programs and add multimedia features to the Internet's World Wide Web. It is similar to the C++ computer programming language and is object-oriented, which means that programs can be created by using many pre-existing components, instead of having to write the entire program from scratch.

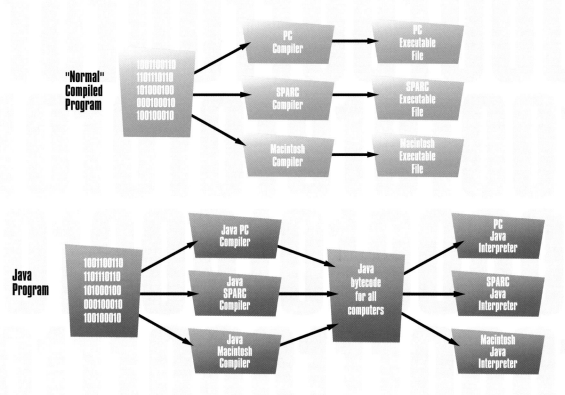

■ Java is a *compiled language*, which means that after a Java program is written the program must be run through a *compiler* in order to turn the program into a language that a computer can read. Java differs from other compiled languages, however. In other compiled languages, computer-specific compilers create distinct executable binary code for all the different computers that the program can run on. In Java, by contrast, a single compiled version of the program—called Java bytecode—is created by a compiler. Interpreters on different computers—such as a PC, Macintosh, or SPARC workstation—understand the Java bytecode and run the program. In this way, a Java program can be created once, and then used on many different kinds of computers. Java programs designed to run inside a Web browser on the World Wide Web are called applets. Java-enabled browsers have Java bytecode interpreters in them.

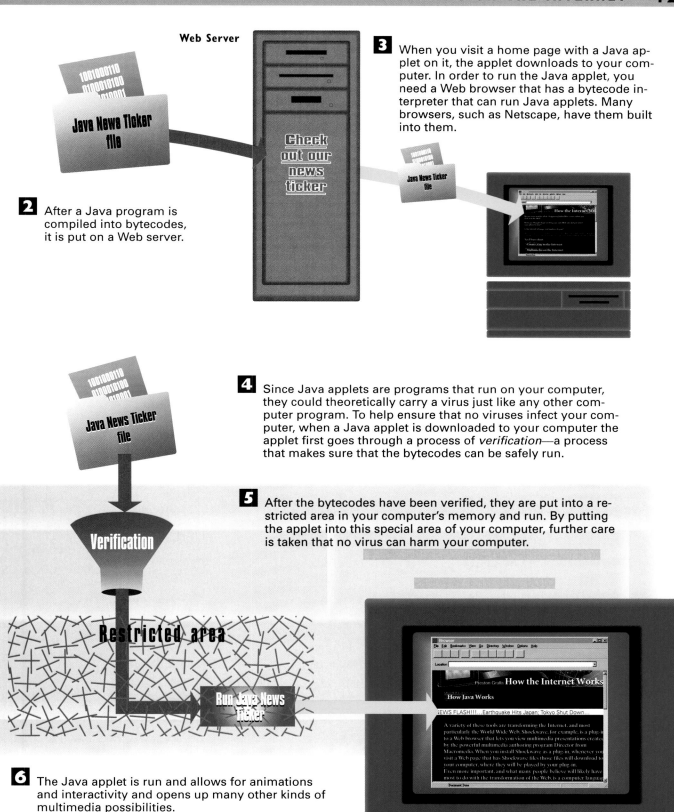

Web Server

2 After a Java program is compiled into bytecodes, it is put on a Web server.

Java News Ticker file

Check out our news ticker

3 When you visit a home page with a Java applet on it, the applet downloads to your computer. In order to run the Java applet, you need a Web browser that has a bytecode interpreter that can run Java applets. Many browsers, such as Netscape, have them built into them.

Java News Ticker file

Java News Ticker file

4 Since Java applets are programs that run on your computer, they could theoretically carry a virus just like any other computer program. To help ensure that no viruses infect your computer, when a Java applet is downloaded to your computer the applet first goes through a process of *verification*—a process that makes sure that the bytecodes can be safely run.

5 After the bytecodes have been verified, they are put into a restricted area in your computer's memory and run. By putting the applet into this special area of your computer, further care is taken that no virus can harm your computer.

Verification

Restricted area

Run Java News Ticker

How the Internet Works

How Java Works

NEWS FLASH!!!...Earthquake Hits Japan; Tokyo Shut Down...

6 The Java applet is run and allows for animations and interactivity and opens up many other kinds of multimedia possibilities.

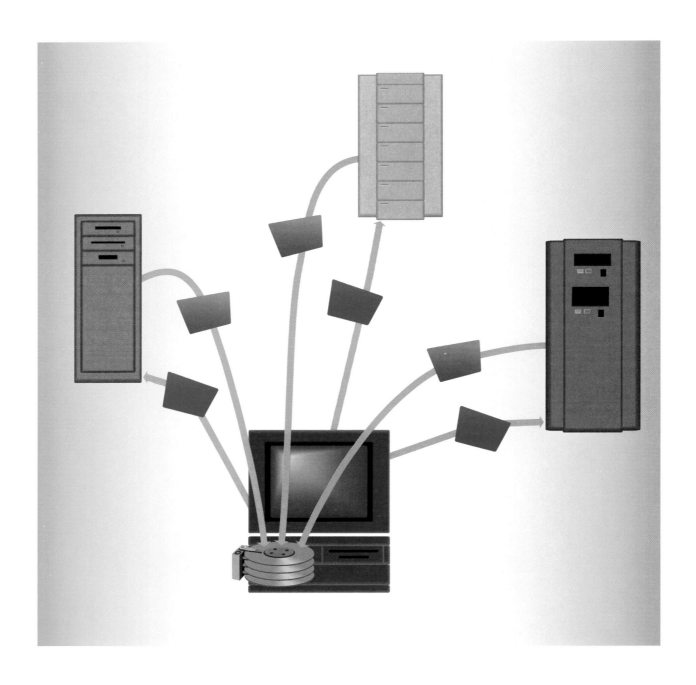

P A R T

APPLYING THE INTERNET

U P until now we've learned about the most important technologies that underlie the Internet—protocols such as TCP/IP, resources such as Telnet, e-mail and the World Wide Web, and multimedia programming tools. In this section of the book, we'll turn our attention to how the Internet is actually being used—in other words, what all those resources, protocols, and tools can do for us.

The reasons that the Internet has grown and become such an important part of our lives is partly due to new technology, and partly due to the many practical uses for the Internet. It has affected almost every aspect of our business lives, and increasingly, our home lives as well. This section of the book looks at many of the ways in which we use the Internet.

In Chapter 23, we'll look at education on the Internet. The Internet began partially as a way to connect universities together, so it should be no surprise that schools and universities remain some of its biggest users. We'll see how the Internet allows for the creation of virtual classrooms and libraries so that students and teachers across the globe can share their work with each other.

Chapter 24 looks at the fastest-growing area of the Internet, and one which shows no sign of slowing down: The use of the Internet for business. One use, a so-called intranet, is growing tremendously. An intranet can be set up by a business for internal communications. A business can put up a firewall around a portion of the Internet that they own. Inside that firewall are corporate e-mail and messaging systems and other corporate computing resources—a kind of private network. Another business use that's growing is shopping on the Internet, which could soon become a multi-billion dollar business.

The Internet may also change the way that health care is practiced. It is already used by researchers and doctors as a way to get at the voluminous amount of medical information available. Patients use the Internet to research their own health problems. Doctors can consult each other long distance, and it may be possible to do surgery remotely over the Internet some day. Chapter 25 explores these applications.

One of the most-cited problems with the Internet is that there's so much information available and so few ways to find it. Chapter 26 explains the different ways the Internet-searching technologies work, from "spiders" to "'bots" to "yellow pages" and indices.

Finally, Chapter 27 examines one of the more intriguing uses of the Internet—the use of so-called agents and daemons. Agents and daemons are programs that launch from your computer, go out across the Internet, and do your bidding for you—for example, gather news or information to display on your computer.

CHAPTER

CHAPTER 23 Education on the Internet

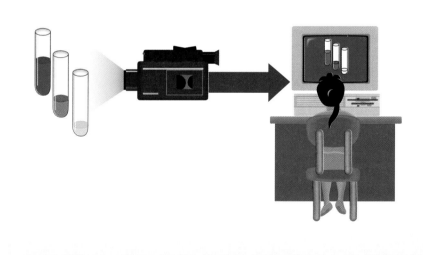

THE Internet was created partly as a way for university researchers to communicate and share their work. Because of that, the Internet has long been used in universities by researchers, professors, and students. Many universities provide Internet accounts for their students. A high percentage of people on the Internet are in fact university students and other people associated with universities. Not only is the Internet used for sharing information and research, but students can now take credit-bearing courses without ever putting foot inside a classroom—they can take courses and tests via the Internet.

Newsgroups allow teachers and students to ask questions, request advice, and share information. Video conferencing technology lets classrooms collaborate on projects. And virtual reality can be used to do things such as allow students to experience what it's like to steer the space shuttle, or let biochemistry researchers create 3-D models of molecules and allow anyone to log into their Web site and see what they've done.

It's not just universities that are using the Internet for education, though. Students in elementary schools, middle schools, and high schools use the Internet for research, for collaborative projects, and for posting their work for the world to see via the World Wide Web.

Libraries are also in the forefront of using the Internet. Many libraries now make their card catalogs available via Telnet so that anyone who can connect to the Internet can search through their collections. And some even go beyond allowing people to search through their catalogs—if you have a library card with that particular library, you can reserve books online as well. Libraries also make available, via the World Wide Web, copies of their special historical collections. For example, the Library of Congress posts many special selections from its historical collections on the World Wide Web—everything from Civil War photographs and journals to posters created by the depression-era Work Projects Administration to photographs of frontier life and Revolutionary-era maps. And libraries increasingly offer access to the Internet—for example, in Cambridge, Massachusetts, anyone can walk into the library and use Macintosh computers and very high-speed Internet connections via cable modem for free.

Museums post their collections as well. Whether you want to browse through the Louvre's world-famous art collection, visit San Francisco's superb Exploratorium, or sample many other museums around the globe, you'll be able to do it via the World Wide Web.

Virtual Education and Research on the Internet

Many libraries allow their entire card catalogs to be accessed on the Internet. Anyone can use Telnet to log into the library's server that contains its card catalog—generally using the same interface and catalog that people use at the library. If a person has a library card at that particular library, some libraries will allow them to reserve books online.

1 Collections of world-famous books are available online and can be downloaded to people's computers and read or printed out. They're usually available as text files. The largest and most well-known of these collections, Project Gutenberg, makes available thousands of copyright-free books, dictionaries, thesauri and other "e-texts," and posts not just plain text versions of the books to download, but also versions that have been created with the Web's markup language, HTML. Project Gutenberg hopes to have 10,000 e-texts available by the end of the year 2001. Project Gutenberg e-texts are available via gopher, WAIS, FTP, and the World Wide Web.

2 Museums around the world use the World Wide Web to post their exhibits online. The Louvre art museum, for example, has posted hundreds of paintings as well as historical, critical, and biographical information about the painters and paintings on the Internet. Anyone can copy the paintings or the information to their own computer.

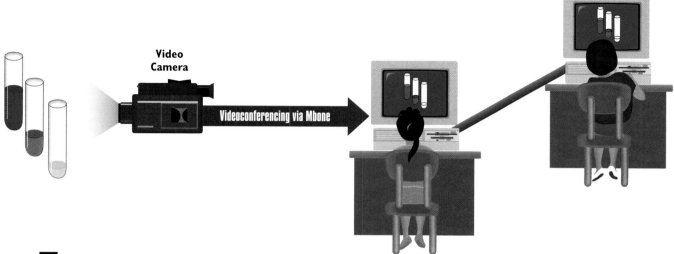

Video Camera

Videoconferencing via Mbone

3 The Internet allows for elementary, grade school, and high school classes to collaborate on projects across the country—or across the world. For example, classes can do environmental research in their own towns, and then post the results on the Web, as well as send the original data to other classes via e-mail or FTP. In the educational site called the Jason Project, students in classrooms around the world tracked how many and what kinds of spiders were in their home towns—and the Jason Project put all the results together, posting them on the Web. Classrooms can also use video conferencing to conduct live discussions about their projects.

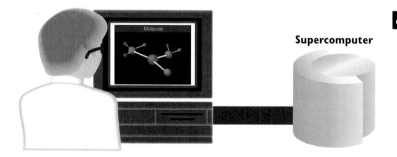

Supercomputer

4 Researchers in biology, chemistry, astronomy, and other disciplines use virtual reality as a way to share the results of their work. Medical researchers have created three-dimensional views of the brain that others can see over the Internet. Chemists have created three-dimensional molecules, and astronomers have three-dimensional views of sections of the universe—and they're all available on the Internet. Scientists can also share information by sending files back and forth, and can use Telnet to log into a supercomputer and use its resources from their own desktop.

5 An enormous number of databases are now available on the Internet, via Telnet, gopher, WAIS, and Web technology. Students, teachers, and researchers can freely tap databases that cover everything from medical information to astronomy.

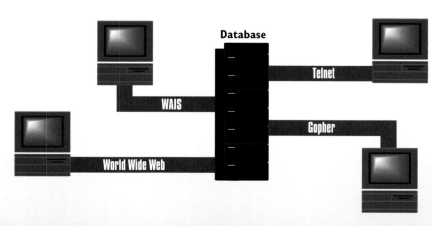

Database

Telnet

WAIS

Gopher

World Wide Web

C H A P T E R
24

Business on the Internet— Introducing Intranets

THE Internet may have its roots in the military and academia, but its dramatic growth has been fueled by business and consumers. The Internet may become one of the primary places that businesses operate, and where billions of dollars of goods and services will be bought and sold every year.

Businesses will increasingly use the Internet in two ways: to market and sell their products and services and accept electronic payment, and to create private corporate networks called *intranets* that will replace current local area networks, and will be corporations' prime computing resources.

As businesses use the Internet to market and sell their products, many people will buy things while at home and from their place of business instead of at retail stores. They will use the Internet to browse through catalogs and make purchases online.

The nature of the Internet is that it's an insecure network. As packets travel across it, anyone along the way could conceivably examine those packets. Because of that, there are potential dangers to doing business online—if you pay over the Internet with a credit card, someone could snoop at it and steal your credit card number and other identifying information.

A number of ways of making payments across the Internet have sprung up to solve the problem. Probably the one that will be most used is the Secure Electronic Transaction protocol (SET)—a set of procedures and protocols designed to make financial transactions on the Internet as confidential as possible. SET uses encryption technology to make sure that no one can steal your credit card number; only the sender and the receiver can decipher the numbers. See Chapter 30 for details on how encryption works. Major credit card companies such as VISA, MasterCard, and American Express support SET, as do software companies such as Microsoft and Netscape. With that backing, SET will almost certainly become the standard way for sending secure credit card information over the Internet.

Corporations can set up intranets for a wide variety of purposes, including e-mail, group brainstorming, group scheduling, access to corporate databases and documents, video conferencing, and more.

Intranets use TCP/IP networks and technologies and Internet resources such as the World Wide Web, e-mail, Telnet, and FTP—but the network and its resources are used privately by businesses, and are not available to people outside the company. An Intranet is separated from the rest of the Internet by a firewall—a hardware and software combination that doesn't allow unauthorized access to the Intranet. People who work in the company can access the Internet and use its resources, but intruders are kept out by the firewalls. See Chapter 28 to learn more about firewalls.

Intranets use a combination of off-the-shelf software such as Web browsers, and customized software such as database querying tools. Since intranets are based on Internet standard protocols, they will always be able to be quickly updated with the latest in network technologies.

How Financial Transactions Work on the Internet

The Internet will increasingly become a place where people can buy goods and services. Before that can happen, though, there must be a secure way for credit card information to be sent over the notoriously insecure Internet. There are many methods for doing this, but one standard, called the Secure Electronic Transaction protocol (SET), will probably be the primary method used. It has been endorsed by VISA, MasterCard, American Express, Microsoft, and Netscape, among other companies. It is a system that will allow people to do secure business over the Internet. This illustration shows how a transaction using SET might work.

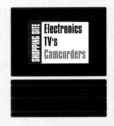

1 Gabriel browses through an electronic catalog on a Web site and he decides to buy a camcorder. In order to use SET to pay for it, he will need a credit card from a participating bank and a unique "electronic signature" for his computer; this will verify that he is making the purchase, not an impostor. (In SET, everyone involved in the transaction needs electronic signatures identifying them.) SET also uses public-key encryption technology to encrypt all the information sent between everyone involved in the transaction.

2 Gabriel fills out an order form detailing what he wants to buy, its price, and any shipping, handling, and taxes. He then selects the method he wants to use to pay. In this case, he decides to pay electronically over the Internet. At this point, he doesn't send his precise credit card number, but instead indicates which credit card he wants to use. The information he sends includes his electronic signature, so that the merchant can verify it is really Gabriel who wants to do the ordering.

3 The merchant receives the order form from Gabriel. A unique transaction identifier is created by the merchant's software, so that the transaction can be identified and tracked. The merchant sends this identifier back to Gabriel along with two "electronic certificates" which are required to complete the transaction for his specific bank card. One certificate identifies the merchant, and the other certificate identifies a specific *payment gateway*—an electronic gateway to the banking system that processes online payments.

4 Gabriel's software receives the electronic certificates and uses them to create Order Information (OI) and Payment Instructions (PI). It encrypts these messages and includes Gabriel's electronic signature in them. The OI and the PI are sent back to the merchant.

"VERIFICATION"

5 The merchant's software decrypts Gabriel's Order Information, and using the electronic signature that Gabriel sent, verifies that the order is from him. The merchant sends verification to Gabriel that the order has been made.

6 The merchant's software creates an authorization request for payment, and includes with the merchant's digital signature the transaction identifier and the Payment Instructions received from Gabriel. He encrypts all of it and sends the encrypted request to the Payment Gateway.

7 The Payment Gateway decrypts the messages and uses the merchant's digital signature to verify that the message is from the merchant. By examining the Payment Instructions, it verifies that they have come from Gabriel. The Payment Gateway then uses a bank card payment system to send an authorization request to the bank which issued Gabriel his bank card, asking if the purchase can be made.

8 When the bank responds that the payment can be made, the Payment Gateway creates, digitally signs, and encrypts an authorization message, which is sent to the merchant. The merchant's software decrypts the message, and uses the digital signature to verify that it comes from the Payment Gateway. Assured of payment, the merchant now ships the camcorder to Gabriel.

9 Some time after the transaction has been completed, the merchant requests payment from the bank. The merchant's software creates a "capture request," which includes the amount of the transaction, the transaction identifier, a digital signature, and other information about the transaction. The information is encrypted and sent to the Payment Gateway.

10 The Payment Gateway decrypts the capture request, and uses the digital signature to verify it is from the merchant. It sends a request for payment to the bank, using the bank card payment system. It receives a message authorizing payment, encrypts the message, and then sends the authorization to the merchant.

"REQUEST FOR PAYMENT"

"PAYMENT AUTHORIZATION"

"PAYMENT AUTHORIZATION"

11 The merchant software decrypts the authorization, verifies that it is from the Payment Gateway, and then stores the authorization which will be used to reconcile the payment when it is received as it normally is in credit card transactions from the bank.

LEGEND

Internet

Order form

Gabriel's digital signature

Merchant digital signature

Payment gateway electronic signature

Unique transaction identifier

Merchant electronic certificate

Payment gateway electronic certificate

Encryption key

Order information

Payment/instructions

Authorization request

Authorization message

Capture request

The Intranet: Using the Internet within a Company

Increasingly, corporations are turning to the Internet as a way to help them run their businesses. They are building intranets—internal corporate networks that work and look just like the Internet, except that they are built for corporate use and are not publicly available to the rest of the Internet.

1 An intranet is separated from the rest of the Internet by a *firewall*—a hardware/software combination that protects the corporate intranet from snooping eyes and malicious attacks. The firewall allows corporate employees to use the Internet, and also allows certain parts of the intranet—such as areas designed for electronic commerce—to be accessed by outsiders.

2 A key component of an intranet is an internal e-mail system. The e-mail system works just like Internet e-mail. It can use normal Internet e-mail clients, except that it is designed to route traffic within an organization, and so the e-mail need not travel outside the intranet. Internal routers and mail servers send the mail to other corporate employees via the intranet. E-mail that travels to and from the Internet from the intranet must go through the firewall.

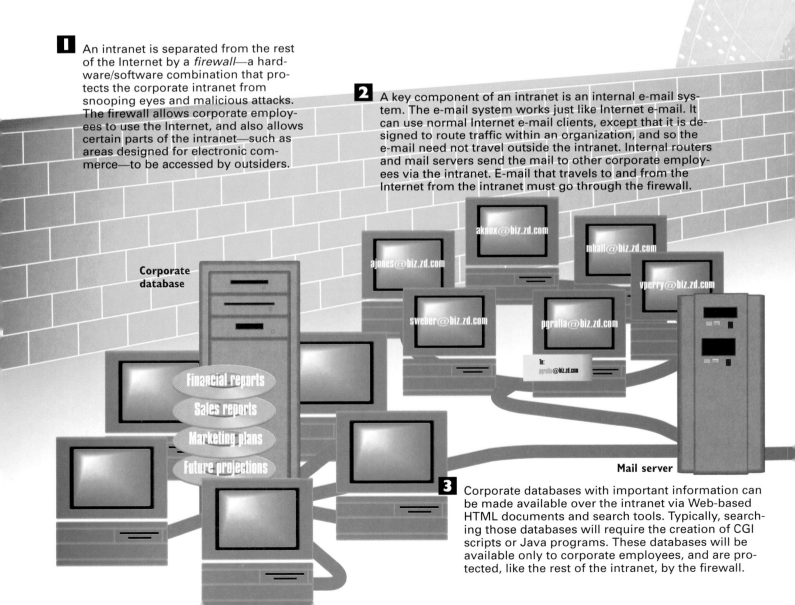

Corporate database

Financial reports
Sales reports
Marketing plans
Future projections

aknox@biz.zd.com
ajones@biz.zd.com
mhall@biz.zd.com
vperry@biz.zd.com
sweber@biz.zd.com
pgralla@biz.zd.com

To:
pgralla@biz.zd.com

Mail server

3 Corporate databases with important information can be made available over the intranet via Web-based HTML documents and search tools. Typically, searching those databases will require the creation of CGI scripts or Java programs. These databases will be available only to corporate employees, and are protected, like the rest of the intranet, by the firewall.

Internet

7 Corporations could allow customers to buy goods and services from them on the Internet by linking the corporation's sales systems to the Internet through the intranet. People could browse through catalogs on the company's public Web site, order goods, and then submit secure payments. The transaction would travel through a firewall in both directions, and would use encryption technology so that it was secure.

Consumers

6 An intranet will make it much easier for a corporation to work with other businesses, such as subcontractors. For example, subcontractors would be able to use a secure Web link into the intranet to submit bids for projects, send invoices, and even receive electronic payment for services. Similarly, employees of the corporation could order parts and services from other businesses using the World Wide Web by sending requests through the firewall to the Internet.

Subcontractor

SECURE LINK

Electronic catalog

Server

Firewall

5 An intranet will also allow corporations to have people regularly attend video conferences—meetings where people in different parts of the country or the world can see and talk to each other using their personal computers. Since the corporation controls the links among business locations, it can create high-speed links specifically for video conferencing—something that would be difficult to do on the wider Internet.

Router

4 An intranet will allow people to collaborate on their work electronically using *groupware*. Groupware allows people to have online brainstorming sessions, schedule group meetings, work on documents and plans together, create common databases, and perform other kinds of cooperative work.

CHAPTER
25

Medicine and the Internet

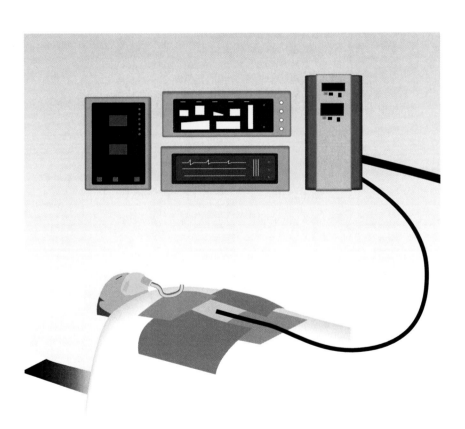

IT may be that the most far-reaching changes to our health care system will come about not because of new legislation or the way insurance companies operate, but instead because of the Internet. The Internet could help revolutionize every aspect of our medical system, from the way doctors are trained, to our access to health care information, and even to the way doctors treat us and operate on us. Health researchers have long shared information via the Internet, by e-mail, postings in newsgroups, and sharing computing resources and files. Because of the ubiquity of the Internet, doctors can now share information as well.

"Virtual hospitals" have already sprung up on the Internet. These hospitals don't actually treat people, but instead they give people easy access to the vast medical resources available on the Internet. Ordinary consumers, for example, can browse and search databases to help them find answers to medical problems. Medical texts and the latest medical findings are posted online to train doctors and make it easier for them to keep up to date with new research.

Many sites devoted to specific health problems have sprung up as well. Web sites devoted to breast cancer, for example, provide information about the disease, its treatment, and allow people who have or have had breast cancer to form online support groups.

What may be the most far-reaching change to the way medicine is performed, however, has to do with what is called *telemedicine*, the use of communications technology—especially the Internet—to allow doctors to practice medicine at a distance from their patients.

Probably the most intriguing use of telemedicine is the use of virtual reality, or telepresence. The virtual reality used in medicine on the Internet is not related to the virtual worlds created by the Internet's VRML language. Instead, it allows doctors to diagnose and treat patients remotely over the Internet—and even do surgery over the Internet using special virtual reality hardware.

Using this technology, a surgeon can be located many miles away from the actual operating room. The doctor will wear virtual reality goggles to give a three-dimensional view inside the patient's body, as well as special gloves that operate a robot, or surgical tools that do the actual operation on a patient. The virtual reality information, as well as instructions for operating the robot, will travel across the Internet. There will be computer technicians at both sites to ensure the equipment operates properly, and nurses and other medical staff in the operating room to prepare the patient for surgery.

Lest you think that using telepresence or virtual reality to practice medicine is a pie-in-the-sky idea, consider this: There are many conferences every year on the subject; many companies have jumped into the field; many researchers are involved in the field; and it's already being done. It's only a matter of time before it becomes even more widespread.

How Virtual Medicine Works on the Internet

Virtual medicine on the Internet will allow a surgeon at one site to operate on a patient at a distant site. This will allow specialized surgeons in major cities to operate on patients in rural areas, providing health care access to those in rural areas who have never had it before. The ability to perform operations remotely is often called *telepresence*.

1 Many people believe that endoscopic surgery is a natural kind of surgery to perform by telepresence. In endoscopic surgery, miniature television cameras and minute surgical instruments enter the body through small incisions. Television cameras relay information to the surgeon to show where to use the surgical tools. This kind of surgery is used on joints, such as the knee or shoulder, and also for chest surgery, gall bladder surgery, and to correct abnormalities of the ovaries. The first step on an endoscopic surgery via telepresence would be to insert the cameras and surgical instruments in the body.

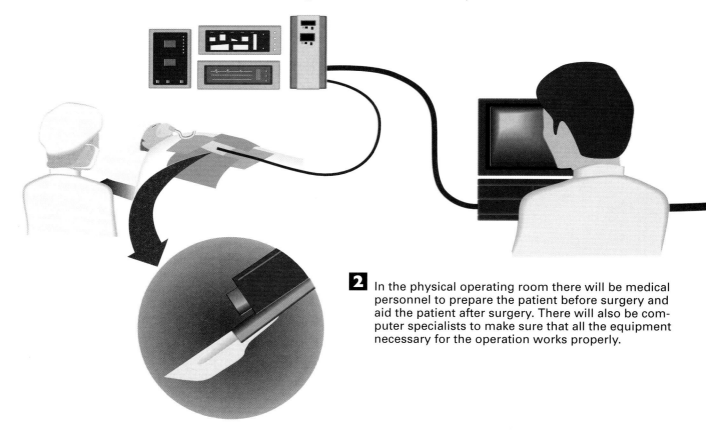

2 In the physical operating room there will be medical personnel to prepare the patient before surgery and aid the patient after surgery. There will also be computer specialists to make sure that all the equipment necessary for the operation works properly.

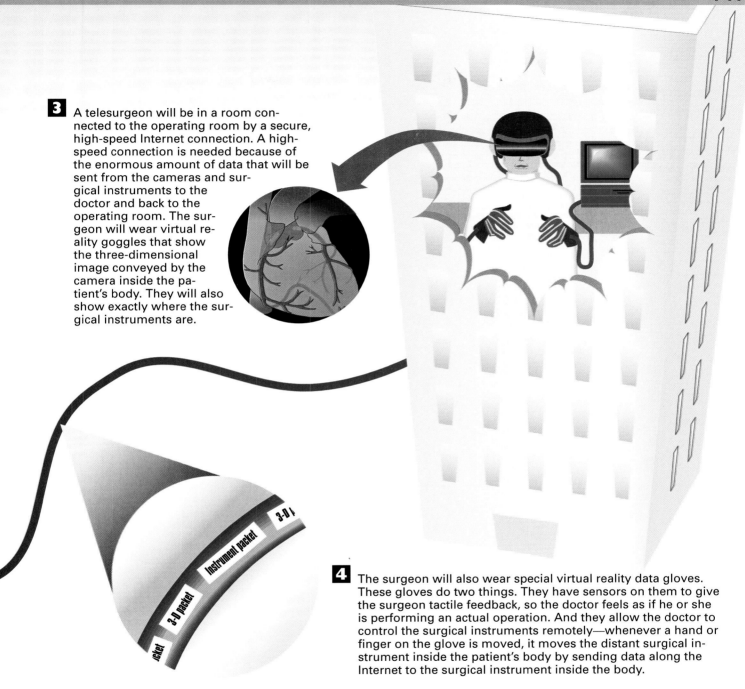

3 A telesurgeon will be in a room connected to the operating room by a secure, high-speed Internet connection. A high-speed connection is needed because of the enormous amount of data that will be sent from the cameras and surgical instruments to the doctor and back to the operating room. The surgeon will wear virtual reality goggles that show the three-dimensional image conveyed by the camera inside the patient's body. They will also show exactly where the surgical instruments are.

4 The surgeon will also wear special virtual reality data gloves. These gloves do two things. They have sensors on them to give the surgeon tactile feedback, so the doctor feels as if he or she is performing an actual operation. And they allow the doctor to control the surgical instruments remotely—whenever a hand or finger on the glove is moved, it moves the distant surgical instrument inside the patient's body by sending data along the Internet to the surgical instrument inside the body.

5 Two sets of information are sent over the Internet to the doctor from inside the patient. Cameras send a data stream that produces the three-dimensional image that is displayed on the doctor's VR goggles. The surgical instruments send information detailing their precise placement and movement. Those data streams are merged on the VR goggles so that the doctor can see inside the body, and also see the location of the instruments.

6 One day doctors may be able to perform other kinds of surgeries, not just endoscopic surgeries, remotely over the Internet. In that case, VR goggles and data gloves would still be used. However, the doctor will not control tiny surgical instruments inside the body, but instead the data gloves will control distant robot arms that perform incisions and do other traditional surgical procedures.

How Agents and CGI Work

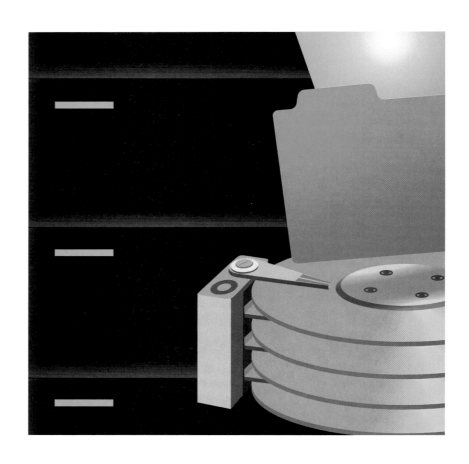

THE Internet has grown so quickly and its resources are so vast that we need help navigating around it. We can now use special software called *agents* to help us access the Net's resources.

While there are a lot of technical definitions for agents, put simply, agents are programs that do your bidding automatically. Agents can run on individual computers or over the Internet. Many agents run on the Internet every day. Agents can find the latest news for you and download it to your computer; they can automatically monitor Internet traffic and report on its total usage; they can find you the best deal on the CD you want to buy; they can perform important Web maintenance tasks; and far more. They are becoming so complex that systems are being developed to allow agents to interact with one another so that they can perform jobs cooperatively.

On the Internet, agents are commonly called spiders (since spiders live on webs, as in the World Wide Web), robots (often shortened to *bots*), and knowbots. Those used for searching automatically create indexes of almost every resource on the Web, and then allow people to search through those indexes to find things more quickly. Common search tools such as Lycos, InfoSeek, and Alta Vista use spiders in this way. We'll cover this specialized use of spiders in Chapter 27.

All of these agents are software programs that are invisible to the user. You just determine the task you want done, and behind the scenes the agent automatically goes off and performs that task. A variety of different languages can be used to write agent programs. One way that agents can be written is to use the Common Gateway Interface, normally referred to as CGI. A number of different agents can be devised in this manner.

CGI, however, can be used for more than just creating agents. If you browse the Web at all, you'll run into CGI programs—usually called CGI scripts—on a regular basis. Essentially, CGI is a standard way in which the Web interacts with outside resources. Often that outside resource is a database. You've probably run CGI scripts many times without knowing it. For example, if you've filled out a form on a Web page in order to register to use a site, and then later received an e-mail notification with a password for you to use, you've probably run a CGI script without knowing it. In that case, the CGI script probably took the information you filled in on the form and performed several actions on it, including putting the information in a database, automatically creating a password, and then sending you mail.

Agents on the Internet

An agent is a program that can automatically go out and perform tasks for you. On the Internet, agents are known by many names, including robots and spiders. They run in the background, unattended. Agents can accomplish many different tasks, such as gathering news for you, shopping for you, and performing important maintenance tasks on Web servers.

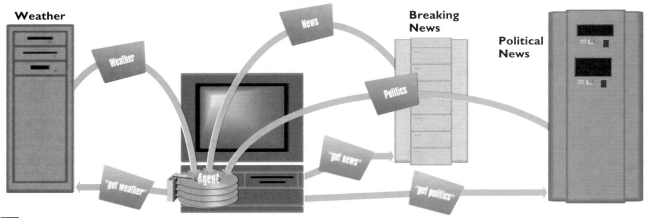

1 A simple Internet agent is one that gathers news from a variety of sources, while you're not using your computer, or while you are using your computer for another task. News agents can work in several ways. In the simplest example, you fill out a form saying what kind of news you're interested in, and on what schedule you want your news delivered. Based on that information, at pre-set intervals, the news agent dials into news sites around the Internet and downloads news stories to your computer, where you can read them as HTML pages.

2 Shopping agents will let you search through all of the Internet for the best bargains. On the Web, you fill out a form detailing the product that you want to buy. When you send the form, the shopping agent launches programs that search through a variety of shopping sites and databases on the Internet. The agent looks into the databases of those sites, and finds the best prices. It then sends the links to the sites back to you, so that you can visit the sites with the best prices and order from there.

4 When robots and spiders do their work on a remote Internet site from where they were launched, they can put extra load on the site's system resources—for example, by swamping the server with too many requests in too short a time. Because of this, some system administrators would like there to be ways to exclude robots in certain circumstances, such as not allowing robots into certain Web directories. A variety of ways have been devised to limit robot access, including creating a file called ROBOTS.TXT that describes the areas off limits to robots, and that the robots would automatically read, adhere to, and not visit.

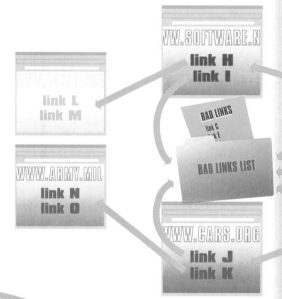

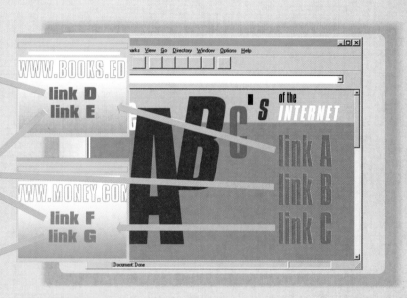

3 Web robots called Web maintenance spiders can perform important Web maintenance chores. On Web sites, particularly large ones, very often HTML pages can include links that become outdated—in other words, the object being linked to has been taken off the Internet. Whenever a user clicks on the link, an error message is sent. A Web maintenance spider can look at every link on every HTML page on a Web site and trace each link to see if the linked object still exists. It then generates a report of dead links. Based on that report, the system administrator can rewrite the HTML code, getting rid of the bad links.

Bargain Place

Hardware Haven

"get best deal"

"get best deal"

How CGI Scripting Works

CGI (Common Gateway Interface) is a standard that allows programmers to write code that can access information servers on the Internet, such as Web servers, and then send the information to users. It's the way that the Web can communicate with outside resources and databases. For example, with CGI, a programmer can write an application on the Web that will let someone search a database of information such as news articles or movies, and then display the information found in home pages in HTML format. CGI is also used to allow people to fill out forms on the Internet—for example, to subscribe to an electronic newsletter. And CGI programs can also be used to construct Web spiders and robots. In our example, we'll look at a CGI program that allows someone to search a movie database for information.

1 People who dial into the Web site don't need to know programming to access CGI programs. Instead, a programmer writes a CGI program. A number of different languages can be used for CGI, such as C or C++, Fortran, Visual Basic, and AppleScript. An application written in a programming language such as C must be first *compiled*—run through a program called a *compiler*—before it can be run. This compiler turns the application into a language that CGI can understand. Other languages, called scripting languages, do not need to be compiled first. CGI scripts tend to be easier to debug, modify, and maintain than compiled programs, and so are used more frequently. Probably the most popular language for writing CGI scripts is Perl.

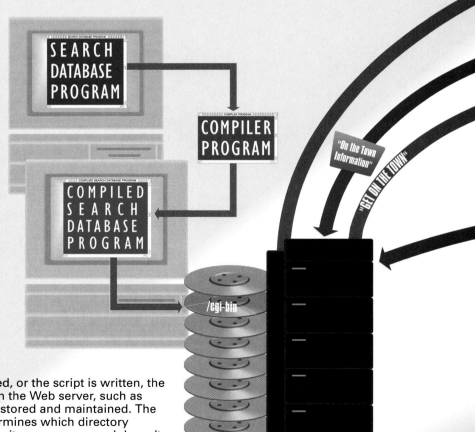

2 After the program is written and compiled, or the script is written, the program is put into a special directory on the Web server, such as /cgi-bin, where all the CGI programs are stored and maintained. The person in charge of the Web server determines which directory should hold CGI programs. If someone writes a program and doesn't put it in the proper directory, it won't run. This is a security feature—if there were many different directories that people could use to store and run CGI programs, it would be difficult to keep track of them all, and someone from the outside could create and post a program that could be dangerous to the software that's already there.

Web Server

6 The CGI program receives the data from the database, and formats it in a way that will be understandable to the user—for example, taking the information and putting it into HTML format so that the user can read it using his or her Web browser. The CGI program sends the results in HTML format to the user, who displays it in a Web browser. The user can now use that HTML page as any other, such as clicking on links to visit other pages, printing it, and viewing graphics and multimedia files.

Database

5 The CGI program contacts a database and requests the information that the user is looking for. The database sends the information to the CGI program. The information can be in a variety of formats, such as text, graphics, sound and video files, and URLs.

4 When you visit the Web site and click on the URL, the CGI program is launched. If the CGI program allows you to search a database, for example, it will send a form in HTML format. You then fill out the form detailing what you want to find. When you finish the form and click on send, the data from the form is sent to the CGI program.

3 After the CGI program is posted to a special directory, a link to it is embedded in a URL on a Web page.

CHAPTER

27 Searching the Internet

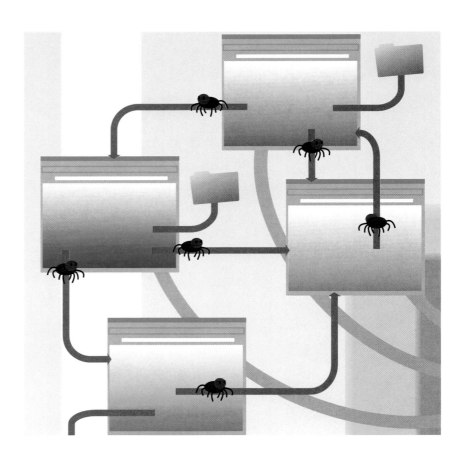

T**HERE** is so much information available on the Internet, and there is so little organization to the Internet, that it can seem impossible to find the information or documents you want. A number of solutions have sprung up to solve the problem. The
two most popular are indexes and search engines.

Indexes present a highly structured way to find information. They let you browse through
information by categories such as arts, computers, entertainment, sports, and so on. In a Web
browser, you click on a category, and you are then presented with a series of subcategories. For
example, under sports you'll find baseball, basketball, football, hockey, and soccer. Depending on
the size of the index, there may be several layers of subcategories. When you get to the subcate-
gory you're interested in, you'll be presented with a list of relevant documents. To get to those
documents, you click on links to them. Yahoo! is the largest and most popular index on the
Internet. Yahoo! and other indexes also let you search through them by typing in words that describe the information you're looking for. You then get a set of search results—links to documents that match your search. To get the information, you click on a link to it.

Another popular way of finding information is to use search engines, also called search tools
and sometimes called Web crawlers. Search engines operate differently from indexes. They are essentially massive databases that cover wide swaths of the Internet. Search engines don't present
information in a hierarchical fashion. Instead, you search through them as you would a database,
by typing in keywords that describe the information you want.

There are many popular Internet search engines, including Lycos, WebCrawler, and Alta
Vista. While the specifics of how they operate differ somewhat, they generally are all composed of
three parts: a *spider,* or spiders, which crawls across the Internet gathering information; a database, which contains all the information that the spiders gather; and a search tool, which people
use to search through the database. Search engines are constantly updated to present the most
up-to-date information, and hold enormous amounts of information. The Alta Vista search engine, for example, crawls across 2.5 million home pages every day. Its database can index text at
the rate of 1 gigabyte of data per hour.

Indexes and search engines make it relatively easy to find information on the Internet, but
it's not so easy to find someone's e-mail address. A system called WHOIS was developed to do
that. It gathers addresses into WHOIS servers that can be searched. However, the system is limited and does not cover many addresses. Other e-mail directory systems, such as the Distributed
Internet Directory, have been tried as well, but they don't work adequately either. For now, finding someone's e-mail address is still extraordinarily difficult.

How Internet Search Engines Work

The Internet is so vast that it can be extremely difficult to find the precise information that you're searching for. To solve the problem, there are a variety of search tools—also called search engines—on the Web. These search tools are commonly called Web spiders or Web crawlers because they "crawl" across the Web and Internet, finding information. Spiders are software programs that travel across the World Wide Web, gathering documents by following the hypertext links found in Web pages. Popular search engines include Lycos, Alta Vista, WebCrawler, and InfoSeek.

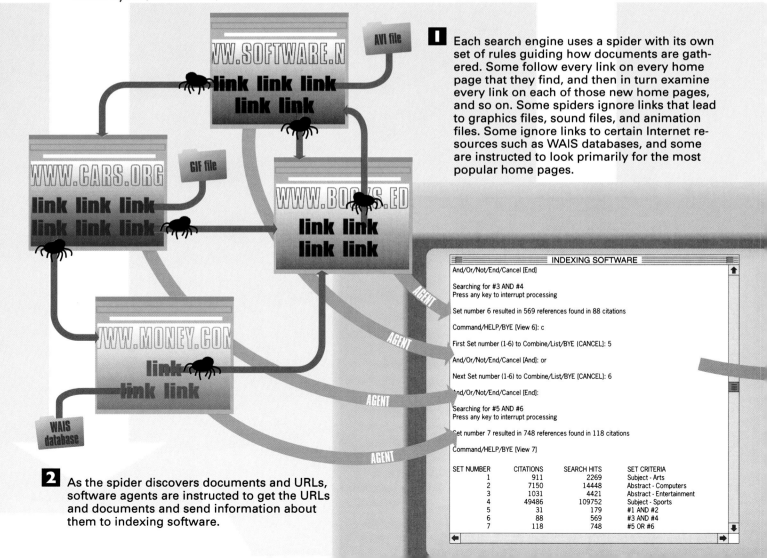

1 Each search engine uses a spider with its own set of rules guiding how documents are gathered. Some follow every link on every home page that they find, and then in turn examine every link on each of those new home pages, and so on. Some spiders ignore links that lead to graphics files, sound files, and animation files. Some ignore links to certain Internet resources such as WAIS databases, and some are instructed to look primarily for the most popular home pages.

2 As the spider discovers documents and URLs, software agents are instructed to get the URLs and documents and send information about them to indexing software.

INDEXING SOFTWARE

And/Or/Not/End/Cancel [End]

Searching for #3 AND #4
Press any key to interrupt processing

Set number 6 resulted in 569 references found in 88 citations

Command/HELP/BYE [View 6]: c

First Set number (1-6) to Combine/List/BYE [CANCEL]: 5

And/Or/Not/End/Cancel [And]: or

Next Set number (1-6) to Combine/List/BYE [CANCEL]: 6

And/Or/Not/End/Cancel [End]:

Searching for #5 AND #6
Press any key to interrupt processing

Set number 7 resulted in 748 references found in 118 citations

Command/HELP/BYE [View 7]

SET NUMBER	CITATIONS	SEARCH HITS	SET CRITERIA
1	911	2269	Subject - Arts
2	7150	14448	Abstract - Computers
3	1031	4421	Abstract - Entertainment
4	49486	109752	Subject - Sports
5	31	179	#1 AND #2
6	88	569	#3 AND #4
7	118	748	#5 OR #6

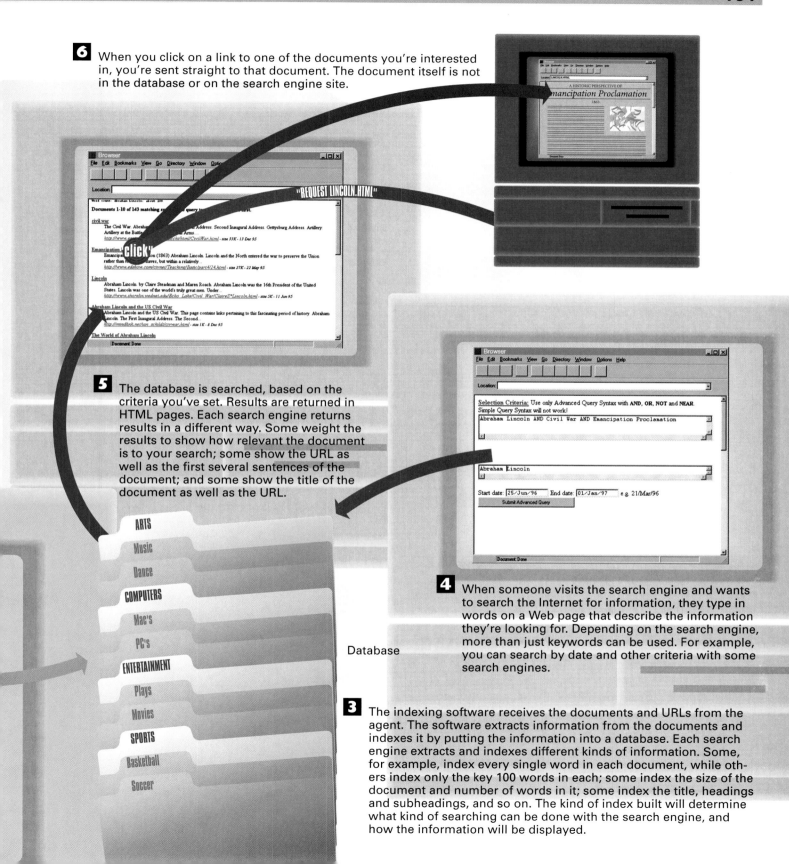

6 When you click on a link to one of the documents you're interested in, you're sent straight to that document. The document itself is not in the database or on the search engine site.

5 The database is searched, based on the criteria you've set. Results are returned in HTML pages. Each search engine returns results in a different way. Some weight the results to show how relevant the document is to your search; some show the URL as well as the first several sentences of the document; and some show the title of the document as well as the URL.

Database

4 When someone visits the search engine and wants to search the Internet for information, they type in words on a Web page that describe the information they're looking for. Depending on the search engine, more than just keywords can be used. For example, you can search by date and other criteria with some search engines.

3 The indexing software receives the documents and URLs from the agent. The software extracts information from the documents and indexes it by putting the information into a database. Each search engine extracts and indexes different kinds of information. Some, for example, index every single word in each document, while others index only the key 100 words in each; some index the size of the document and number of words in it; some index the title, headings and subheadings, and so on. The kind of index built will determine what kind of searching can be done with the search engine, and how the information will be displayed.

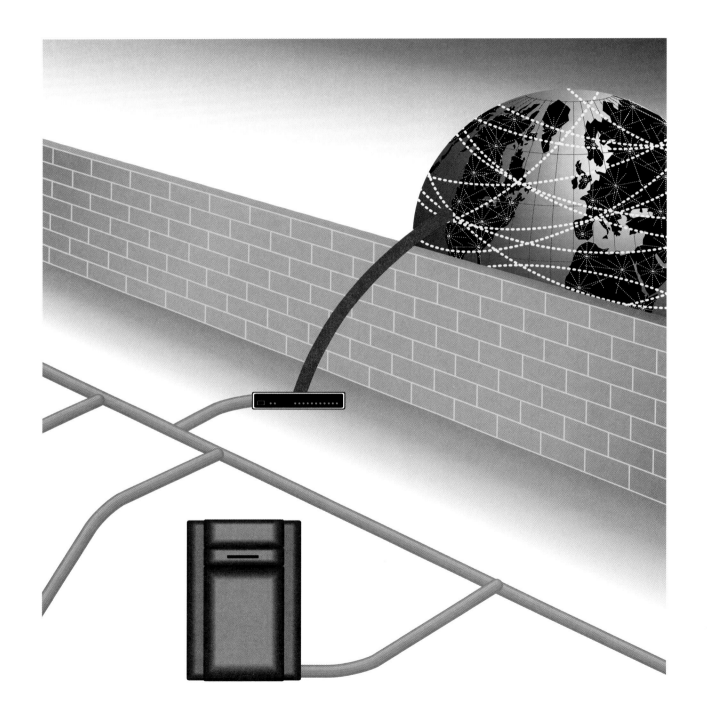

P A R T

SAFEGUARDING THE INTERNET

THE very nature of the Internet makes it vulnerable to attack. It was designed to allow for the freest possible exchange of information, data, and files—and it has succeeded admirably, far beyond its designers' wildest expectations. But that freedom carries a price: hackers and virus-writers try to attack the Internet and computers connected to the Internet; those who want to invade others' privacy attempt to crack into databases of sensitive information or snoop on information as it travels across Internet routes; and some of the information being freely exchanged on the Internet is pornographic.

In this section of the book, we'll look at a variety of security-related issues. We'll see how a variety of tools has been developed for making transactions on the Net more secure, and helping companies protect their sensitive data. We'll also examine the thorny issue of pornography versus free speech, and we'll see how software can block children from visiting obscene sites or getting obscene materials.

Chapter 28 looks at how firewalls work. Many companies whose networks are connected to the Internet have a great deal of sensitive information on their networks, and want to make sure that their data and computers are safe from attack. The answer is to use firewalls—systems that allow people from inside a company to use the Internet, but that stop people on the Internet from getting at the company's computers.

Chapter 29 looks at how viruses work—and how they are detected as well. Any program that you download from the Internet has the potential for being infected with a virus, and it could in turn infect your computer. We'll see just how these nasty data-killers work, and we'll look at anti-virus tools that can detect and kill them.

In Chapter 30 we'll examine cryptosystems. An enormous amount of information is sent across the Internet every day—everything from personal e-mail to corporate data, to credit card information and other highly sensitive material. All that information is vulnerable to hackers and snoopers. Since the information is sent in packets along public routers, there is the possibility that someone could intercept and decipher it. As a way to ensure that the sensitive material can't be looked at, sophisticated cryptosystems have been developed so that only the sender and receiver know what's in the packets.

Finally, Chapter 31 takes a detailed look at the issues around pornography and free speech on the Internet. Explicit sexual material is posted on the Internet, and there are those who would fine and jail people and organizations that allow such material to be posted. Passing those kinds of laws raises a whole host of constitutional issues around free speech. As a way to solve the problem, companies create and sell software for parents that allows them to block their children from seeing obscene and violent material on the Internet. We'll see in detail how one of the most popular pieces of parental control software works.

CHAPTER

28

How Firewalls Work

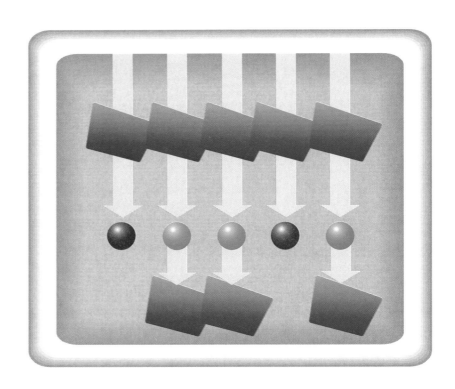

EVERY time a corporation connects its internal computer network to the Internet it faces potential danger. Because of the Internet's openness, every corporate network connected to it is vulnerable to attack. Hackers on the Internet could theoretically break into the corporate network and do harm in a number of ways: steal or damage important data; damage individual computers or the entire network; use the corporate computer's resources; or use the corporate network and resources as a way of posing as a corporate employee.

The solution isn't to cut off the network from the Internet. Instead, the company can build firewalls to protect their network from attack. These firewalls allow anyone on the corporate network to access the Internet, but they stop hackers or others on the Internet from gaining access to the corporate network and causing damage.

Firewalls are hardware and software combinations that are built using routers, servers, and a variety of software. They sit at the most vulnerable point between a corporate network and the Internet, and they can be as simple or complex as system administrators want to build them. There are many different types of firewalls, but most of them have a few common elements.

One of the simplest kinds of firewalls employs *packet filtering*. In packet filtering, a *screening router* examines the header of every packet of data traveling between the Internet and the corporate network. Packet headers have information in them, including the IP address of the sender and receiver, the protocol being used to send the packet, and other similar information. Based on that information, the router knows what kind of Internet service (such as FTP or rlogin) is being used to send the data, as well as the identity of the sender and receiver of the data. Based on that, the router can bar certain packets from being sent between the Internet and the corporate network. For example, the router could block any traffic except for e-mail, or could block traffic to and from suspicious destinations.

Other common components of firewalls are *bastion hosts*. These are servers that handle all incoming requests from the Internet to the corporate network such as FTP requests. Bastion hosts are heavily fortified against attack. By having only a single host handle incoming requests, it is easier to maintain security and track attacks—and in the event of a break-in, only that single host has been compromised, not the entire network.

Proxy servers are also commonly used in firewalls. When someone inside the corporate network wants to access a server on the Internet, a request from the computer is sent to the proxy server, the proxy server contacts the server on the Internet, and then the proxy server sends the information from the Internet server to the computer inside the corporate network. By acting as a go-between, proxy servers can maintain security as well as log all traffic between the Internet and the network.

How Firewalls Work

Firewalls are combined hardware and software systems that protect corporate networks from malicious attacks launched from someone using the Internet. They are designed to stop intruders from breaking into the corporate network, as well as to stop users on the internal corporate network from accessing any Internet resources that may prove harmful to the network. There are many kinds of firewalls. The one pictured here uses a screened subnet architecture, a particularly secure kind of firewall.

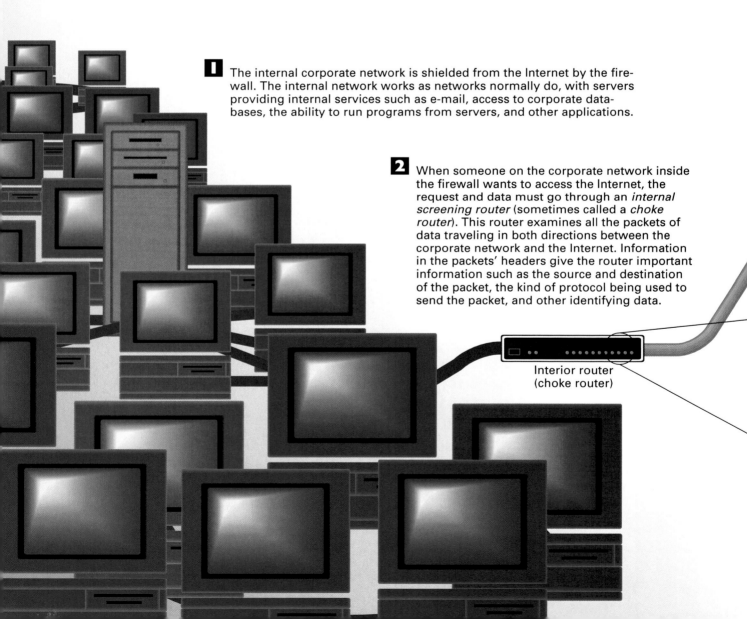

1 The internal corporate network is shielded from the Internet by the firewall. The internal network works as networks normally do, with servers providing internal services such as e-mail, access to corporate databases, the ability to run programs from servers, and other applications.

2 When someone on the corporate network inside the firewall wants to access the Internet, the request and data must go through an *internal screening router* (sometimes called a *choke router*). This router examines all the packets of data traveling in both directions between the corporate network and the Internet. Information in the packets' headers give the router important information such as the source and destination of the packet, the kind of protocol being used to send the packet, and other identifying data.

Interior router
(choke router)

Internet

6 An *exterior screening router* (also called an *access router*) screens packets between the Internet and the perimeter network. It adds an extra level of protection: It screens packets based on the same rules as the internal screening router and so will protect the network even if the internal router fails. It also, however, may add more rules for screening packets specifically designed to protect the bastion host.

Firewall

5 The bastion host is placed in a *perimeter network* in the firewall, so it is not on the corporate network itself. This further shields the corporate network from the Internet. If the bastion host was on the normal corporate network, an intruder could conceivably gain access to every computer on the network and to all network services. By isolating the bastion server from the corporate network by putting it in a perimeter network, even if the server is broken into, the intruder still can't gain access to the internal corporate network.

Exterior router
(access router)

Bastion host

4 A *bastion host* in the firewall is the primary point of contact for connections coming in from the Internet for services such as receiving e-mail and allowing access to the corporation's FTP site. The bastion host is a heavily protected server with many security provisions built in, and it is the only contact point for incoming Internet requests. In this way, none of the computers or hosts on the corporate network can be contacted directly for requests from the Internet, providing a level of security. Bastion hosts can also be set up as proxy servers—servers that process any requests from the internal corporate network to the Internet, such as browsing the Web or downloading files via FTP. See the next illustration for an explanation of how proxy servers work.

Internal
network

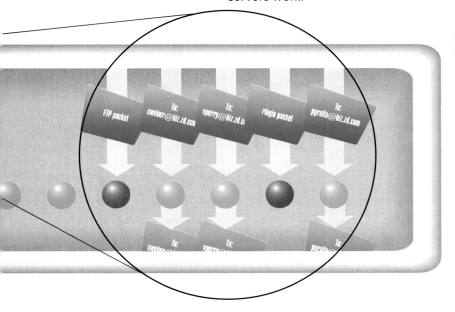

3 Based on the information in the headers, the screening router will allow certain packets to be sent or received, but will block other packets. For example, it might not allow some services such as rlogin to be run. (The command, rlogin, is similar to Telnet, allowing someone to log into a computer. It can be dangerous because it allows users to bypass having to type in a password.) The router also might not allow any packets to be sent to and from specific Internet locations because those locations have been found to be suspicious. Conceivably, a router could be set up to block every packet traveling between the Internet and the internal network except for e-mail. System administrators set the rules for determining which packets to allow in and which to block.

How Proxy Servers Work

A proxy server is server software that runs on a host in a firewall—such as a bastion host—that acts as a go-between among computers on a protected network and the Internet. Because only the single proxy server—instead of the many individual computers on the network—interacts with the Internet, security can be maintained. That single server can be kept more secure than can hundreds of individual computers on a network.

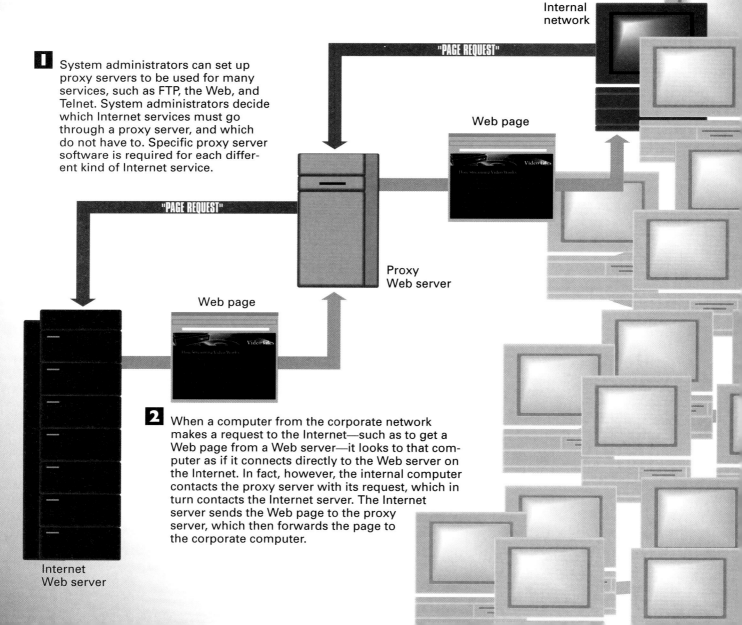

1 System administrators can set up proxy servers to be used for many services, such as FTP, the Web, and Telnet. System administrators decide which Internet services must go through a proxy server, and which do not have to. Specific proxy server software is required for each different kind of Internet service.

Internal network

"PAGE REQUEST"

Web page

Proxy Web server

"PAGE REQUEST"

Web page

2 When a computer from the corporate network makes a request to the Internet—such as to get a Web page from a Web server—it looks to that computer as if it connects directly to the Web server on the Internet. In fact, however, the internal computer contacts the proxy server with its request, which in turn contacts the Internet server. The Internet server sends the Web page to the proxy server, which then forwards the page to the corporate computer.

Internet Web server

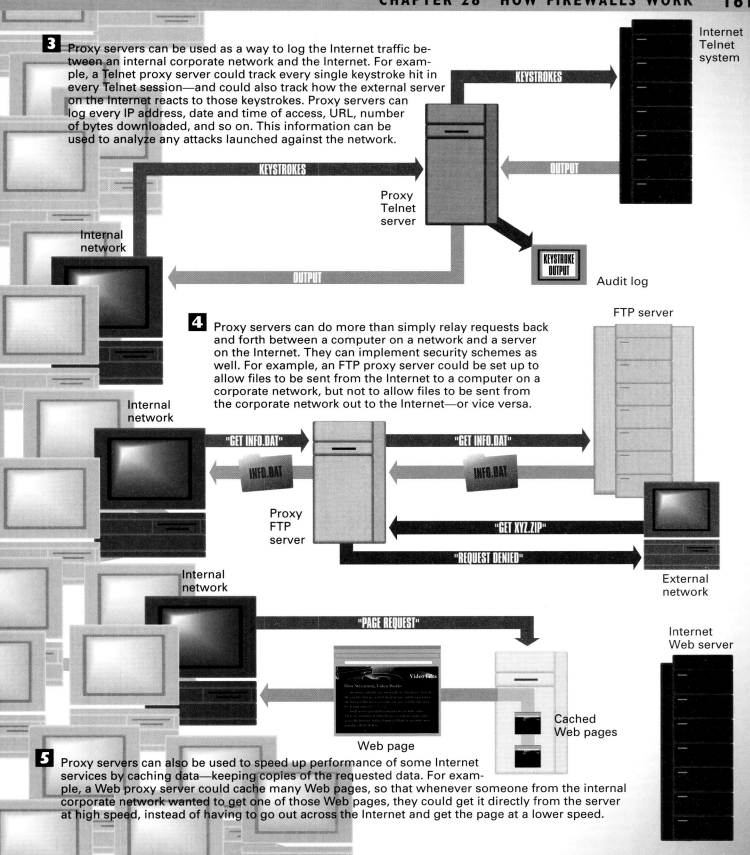

3 Proxy servers can be used as a way to log the Internet traffic between an internal corporate network and the Internet. For example, a Telnet proxy server could track every single keystroke hit in every Telnet session—and could also track how the external server on the Internet reacts to those keystrokes. Proxy servers can log every IP address, date and time of access, URL, number of bytes downloaded, and so on. This information can be used to analyze any attacks launched against the network.

Internet Telnet system

KEYSTROKES

OUTPUT

Proxy Telnet server

KEYSTROKES

Internal network

OUTPUT

KEYSTROKE OUTPUT

Audit log

4 Proxy servers can do more than simply relay requests back and forth between a computer on a network and a server on the Internet. They can implement security schemes as well. For example, an FTP proxy server could be set up to allow files to be sent from the Internet to a computer on a corporate network, but not to allow files to be sent from the corporate network out to the Internet—or vice versa.

FTP server

Internal network

"GET INFO.DAT"

"GET INFO.DAT"

INFO.DAT

INFO.DAT

Proxy FTP server

"GET XYZ.ZIP"

"REQUEST DENIED"

External network

Internal network

"PAGE REQUEST"

Internet Web server

Video Files

How Streaming Video Works

Cached Web pages

Web page

5 Proxy servers can also be used to speed up performance of some Internet services by caching data—keeping copies of the requested data. For example, a Web proxy server could cache many Web pages, so that whenever someone from the internal corporate network wanted to get one of those Web pages, they could get it directly from the server at high speed, instead of having to go out across the Internet and get the page at a lower speed.

CHAPTER

29

How Viruses Work

$\mathbf{T}\textsf{HE}$ Internet, just like the rest of the world, is not a perfectly safe place to visit. If you download files from the Internet, there is a chance— a very small chance, but nonetheless a chance—that your computer could become infected with a virus.

Viruses are malicious programs that invade your computer. They can cause many different kinds of damage, such as deleting data files, erasing programs, or destroying everything they find on your hard disk. Not every virus causes damage; some simply flash annoying messages on your screen. But whenever you have a virus, you'll want to eradicate it.

While you can get a virus from the Internet by downloading files to your computer, the Internet is not the only place that viruses can be picked up. They can also infect files on online services, computer bulletin board systems, local area networks, and even shrink-wrapped software that you buy in a retail store.

The term "virus" is a somewhat generic term applied to a wide variety of programs. Traditional viruses attach themselves to programs or data files, infect your computer, replicate themselves on your hard disk, and then damage your data, hard disk, or files. Viruses usually attack four parts of your computer: its executable program files; its file-directory system that tracks the location of all of your computer's files (and without which, your computer won't work); its boot and system areas that are needed in order to start your computer; and its data files. There was a time when it was believed that data files could not be infected by viruses, but recently viruses have been written that infect data files too. Some viruses, for example, attach themselves to Word for Windows macros inside a Word for Windows data file, and are launched whenever a particular macro is run.

Trojan horses are programs that disguise themselves as normal, helpful programs, but in fact damage your computer, its data, or your hard disk. For example, if a program purported to be a financial calculator, but really deleted every file on your hard disk ending in .DOC, that program would be called a Trojan horse.

Worms are programs designed to infect networks such as the Internet. They travel from networked computer to networked computer, replicating themselves along the way. The most infamous worm of all was released on November 2, 1988, and copied itself to many Internet host computers, eventually bringing the Internet to its knees.

The best way to protect your computer against viruses is to use anti-viral software. There are several kinds. A *scanner* checks to see if your computer has any files that have been infected, while an *eradication program* will wipe the virus from your hard disk. Sometimes eradication programs can kill the virus without having to delete the infected program or data file, while other times those infected files must be deleted. Still other programs, sometimes called *inoculators*, will not allow a program to be run if it contains a virus, and stops your computer from being infected.

How Viruses Infect Computers

Your computer can get a virus from the Internet if you download software or other kinds of files to your own computer. Viruses are written for specific kinds of computers, such as PCs or Macintoshes, because the files they infect will run only on one kind of computer. Until recently, it was thought that viruses could infect only program files. Now, however, it has been discovered that some viruses can infect data files as well.

3 Viruses can corrupt program or data files so that they work oddly, not at all, or cause damage when they do run. They can destroy all the files on your computer, change the system files that your computer needs when it is turned on, and cause other types of damage.

Virus

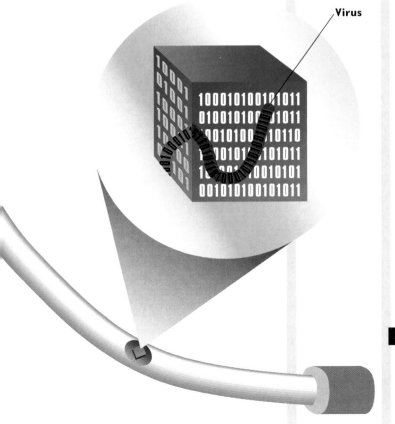

1 A virus hides inside a legitimate program where it remains dormant until you run the infected program. The virus springs into action when you actually run the infected program. Sometimes the first thing the virus will do is infect other programs on your hard disk by copying itself into them.

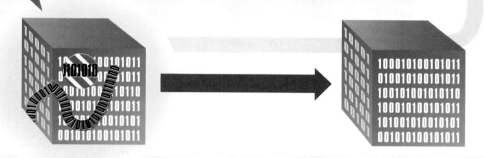

5 Eradication programs disinfect, or remove, viruses from software. Sometimes they can eradicate the virus without damaging the program which the virus has infected. In other instances, they have to destroy the program as well as the virus.

4 Software programs called scanners check for viruses and alert you to viruses' presence. They work in many different ways. One method of detection is to check your program files for tell-tale virus markers that indicate the presence of a virus. Other methods include checking to see whether a program's file size has changed. Some types of anti-viral programs run continuously on your computer, and check any program for the presence of a virus before the program is run.

Virus marker

2 Some viruses place messages called *v-markers* or *virus markers* inside programs that they infect, and these help manage the viruses' activities. Each virus has a specific virus marker associated with it. If a virus encounters one of these markers in another program, it knows that the program is already infected, and so it doesn't replicate itself there. When a virus cannot find any more unmarked files on a computer, that can signal to the virus that there are no more files to be infected. At this point, the virus may begin to damage the computer and its data.

CHAPTER 30

Cryptography and Privacy

EVERY packet of data sent over the Internet traverses many public networks. At any step of the way, many people could have access to those packets, so they are not private. However, the Internet is also used for transmitting highly confidential information, such as corporate data and credit card numbers. Unless there is some way to protect that kind of confidential information, the Internet will never be a secure place to do business or send private, personal correspondence.

Software engineeers have developed ways to send confidential information securely. The information needs to be *encrypted*—that is, altered so that to anyone other than the intended recipient it will look like meaningless garble. And the information also needs to be *decrypted*—that is, turned back into the original message by the recipient, and only by the recipient. Many complex systems have been created to allow for this kind of encryption and decryption, and they are called *cryptosystems*.

The heart of understanding how cryptosystems work is to understand the concept of *keys*. Keys are secret values that are used by computers in concert with complex mathematical formulas called algorithms to encrypt and decrypt messages. The idea behind keys is that if someone encrypts a message with a key, only someone with a matching key will be able to decrypt the message.

There are two kinds of common encryption systems: *secret-key cryptography*, also called symmetric cryptography, and *public-key cryptography*, also called asymmetric cryptography. The most common secret-key cryptography system is the Data Encryption Standard (DES). The best known public-key system is known as RSA.

In secret-key cryptography, only one key is used to encrypt and decrypt messages. Both the sender and the receiver need to have copies of the same secret key. By contrast, in public-key cryptography, two keys are involved: a public key and a private key. Every person has both a public key and a private key. The public key is made freely available, while the private key is kept secret on the person's computer. The public key can encrypt messages—but only the private key can decrypt messages that the public key has encrypted. If someone wanted to send a message to you, for example, he or she would encrypt them with your public key. But only you, with your private key, would be able to decrypt the message and read it. Your public key could not decrypt it.

It's not feasible to use private-key cryptosystems widely on the Internet for things such as electronic commerce. For a company to conduct business over the Internet with a private-key system, it would mean creating millions of different private keys—one for each person who wanted to do business—and then figuring out some way to send those private keys securely over the Internet. With a public-key system, the business only needs to create a single public/private key combination. The business would post the public key for anyone to use to encrypt information—but only the business itself, with the private key, would be able to decrypt the data.

How Cryptosystems Work

Because of the open nature of the Internet, it is easy for people to intercept messages that travel across it—making it difficult to send confidential messages or financial data such as credit card information. To solve the problem, cryptosystems have been developed. A popular one, called RSA, uses *keys* to encrypt and decrypt messages so that only the sender and receiver can understand the messages. The system requires that each person have a *public key* that is made available to anyone, and a *private key* that they keep only on their computer. Data encrypted with someone's private key can only be decrypted with their public key; and data encrypted with their public key can only be decrypted with their private key. This illustration is an example of how a public-key system works. In it, Gabriel and Mia want to exchange a confidential message. They have already exchanged public keys.

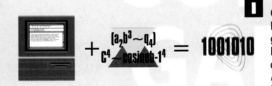

1 Gabriel wants to send a confidential message over the Internet to Mia. Mia will need some way to decrypt the message—as well as a way to guarantee that the message has been actually sent by Gabriel, and not by an impostor. First, Gabriel runs his message through an algorithm called a *hash function*. This produces a number known as the *message digest*. The message digest acts as a sort of "digital fingerprint" that Mia will use to ensure that no one has altered the message.

2 Gabriel now uses his private key to encrypt the message digest. This produces a unique digital signature that only he, with his private key, could have created.

3 Gabriel generates a new random key. He uses this key to encrypt his original message and his digital signature. Mia will need a copy of this random key in order to decrypt Gabriel's message. This random key is the only key in the world that can decrypt the message—and at this point only Gabriel has the key.

4 Gabriel encrypts this new random key with Mia's public key. This encrypted random key is referred to as the *digital envelope*. Only Mia will be able to decrypt the random key since it was encrypted with her public key—and so only her private key can decrypt it.

5 Gabriel sends a message over the Internet to Mia that is composed of several parts: the encrypted confidential message, the encrypted digital signature, and the encrypted digital envelope.

6 Mia gets the message. She decrypts the digital envelope with her private key—and out of it gets the random key that Gabriel used to encrypt the message.

Original message

Hash function

7 Mia uses the random key to decrypt Gabriel's message. She can now read the confidential message that he sent to her. She can't yet be sure, however, that the message hasn't been altered en route—or that the message was in fact sent by Gabriel.

1001010
Message digest

Gabriel's public key

8 She now uses Gabriel's public key to decrypt his encrypted digital signature. When she does this, she gets his message digest—the message's "digital fingerprint."

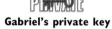
Gabriel's private key

Mia's public key

Mia's private key

9 Mia will use this message digest to see whether the message was in fact sent by Gabriel, and not altered in any way. She takes the message that she had decrypted and runs it through the same algorithm—the hash function—that Gabriel ran the message through. This will produce a new message digest.

Digital signature

Random key

10 Mia compares the message digest that she calculated to the one that she got out of Gabriel's digital signature. If the two match precisely, she can be sure that Gabriel signed the message and that it was not altered after he composed it. If they don't match, then she knows that either he didn't compose the message, or that someone altered the message after he wrote it.

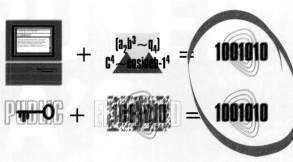

Encrypted message

Encrypted digital signature

Encrypted random key (digital envelope)

C H A P T E R

31

Pornography and Parental Controls

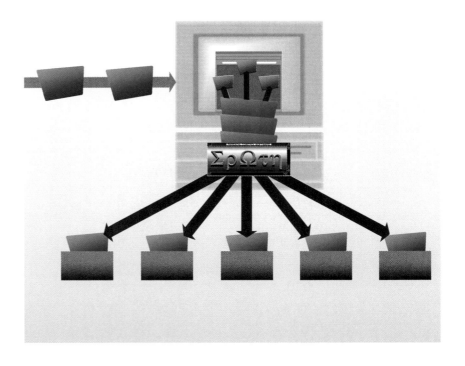

THE very nature of the Internet—the way it allows the free, unfettered flow of information among people—has gotten it a lot of bad publicity. Much has been made of the fact that erotic and pornographic information is available on the Internet, everything from pictures to discussions about subjects that many people find objectionable.

The truth is, that kind of content makes up a very small part of what's available on the Internet. And the objectionable content is not exactly in public view—you have to do a bit of digging to find it.

However, just the fact that it is available to anyone who wants to see it, including children, has made people uncomfortable, so much so that Congress, among others, is taking steps to ban certain kinds of content from being available on the Internet.

The real answer to the problem, though, doesn't lie in legislation, because even if such laws are held to be constitutional, anyone who truly understands the Internet and its technology also recognizes that the laws are unenforceable. The real answer lies with technology itself: software that will allow parents to make sure that their children are not seeing objectionable material.

A number of companies make and sell software that will do this, such as SurfWatch, CyberNanny, and CyberPatrol. They don't all work alike, but they check sites for content, and then bar children from getting at those sites with content that is unsuitable for them.

Online services such as CompuServe, America Online, and Prodigy have a variety of ways to block access to objectionable material on the Internet. Some allow parents to block children from using services such as the World Wide Web, chat, or newsgroups completely. Others, such as America Online, license technology from software makers like those that manufacture SurfWatch to allow anyone on their service to block Internet sites they don't want their children to visit.

One group working on the issue is PICS (Platform for Internet Content Selection), which is trying to give parents control over the kind of material that their children have access to. The group is trying to develop industry standards for technology that would allow the content of all sites and documents on the Internet to be rated according to its suitability for children. They would also create standards that would allow software to be developed that would be able to block sites based on those suitability ratings. Their rating system is also knows as PICS.

Businesses are also concerned with what Internet material their workers are accessing over corporate networks. There is a feeling that if they are getting at and displaying sexual material it could be interpreted as sexual harassment. And, of course, some companies simply don't want their workers accessing that material on company time. Many companies now lease the same software that parents are buying. Instead of installing the software on individual computers, though, the software is installed on a server, and it checks all incoming Internet traffic to every computer in the company.

How Parental Controls Work

Software that allows parents to block their children from accessing parts of the Internet that contain sexual or objectionable material is often called parental control software. This software is installed directly on the computer that the family uses, and blocks objectionable sites from being accessed. There are many different kinds of parental control software. This illustration shows how one of the first and most popular ones works—SurfWatch.

1 SurfWatch software is installed on a computer that a parent wants to monitor to make sure that children can't get at objectionable material on the Internet. When a child launches software to get onto the Internet, SurfWatch latches onto WinSock or MacTCP, depending on whether a PC or a Macintosh is being used. A SurfWatch software module sits "in front" of WinSock or MacTCP (which we'll generically call a TCP/IP stack) and monitors the TCP/IP data stream coming to the TCP/IP stack from the Internet.

2 The SurfWatch module examines the URL of every address coming toward the TCP/IP stack. It looks specifically for five kinds of URLs: https, nntps, ftps, gophers, and IRCs. It takes each of those five types of URLs and puts them each in their own separate "boxes." It allows the rest of the Internet information coming in to go through. SurfWatch checks for these types of URLs since they are the ones that are the most likely to contain objectionable material.

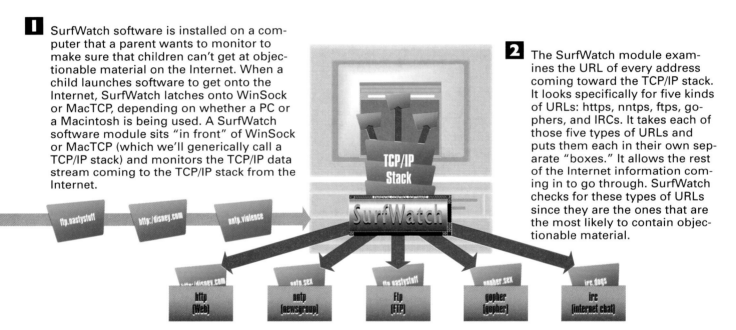

3 Every URL in each of the boxes is checked against a database of the URLs of objectionable sites. If SurfWatch finds that any of the URLs are from objectionable sites, it won't allow that information to be passed on to the TCP/IP stack, blocking the site and preventing information from being viewed. It alerts the child that the site has been blocked. SurfWatch checks thousands of sites, and lists several thousand in its database that it finds objectionable.

4 If the URL is not in the database, SurfWatch does another check of the URL called pattern matching. It looks at the words in the URL itself, and checks them against a database of words to see if they contain certain words that may indicate a request for objectionable material. Often, people creating objectionable material put representative words in the URL itself to draw attention to the site. If SurfWatch finds a matching pattern, it won't allow that information to be passed on to the TCP/IP stack, blocking the site and information from being viewed. It alerts the child that the site has been blocked.

5 There is another way that SurfWatch may eventually check for objectionable sites. A rating system called PICS (Platform for Internet Content Selection) is being developed that will embed information about the content in its documents—saying, for example, whether objectionable material can be found there. If SurfWatch uses this system and finds that the URL is of a site that contains objectionable material, it won't allow that information to be passed on to the TCP/IP stack, blocking the site and information from being viewed. It alerts the child that the site has been blocked.

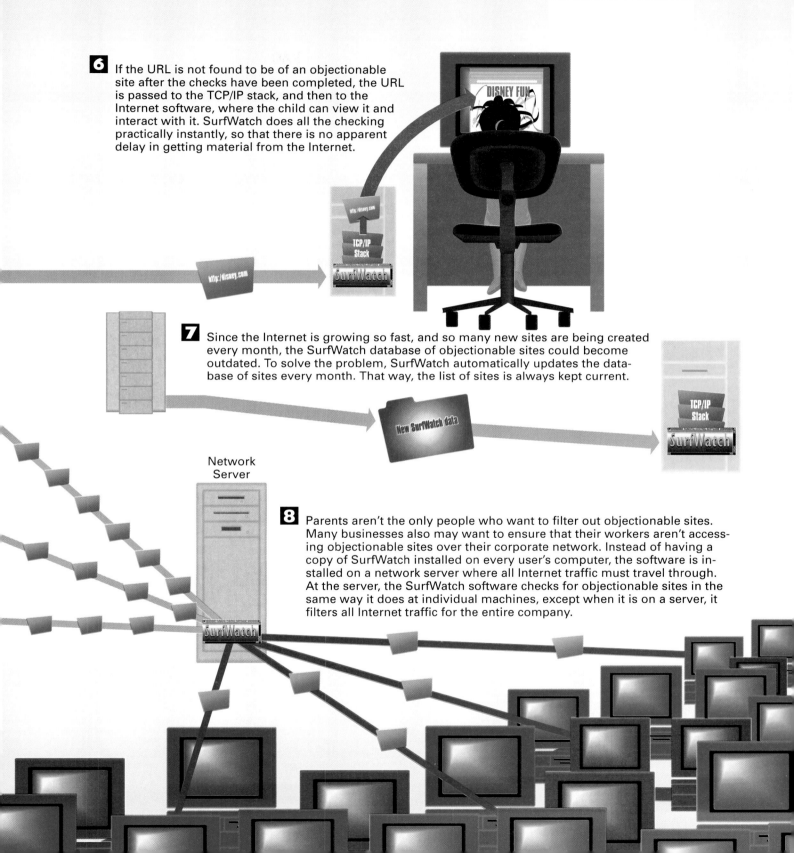

6 If the URL is not found to be of an objectionable site after the checks have been completed, the URL is passed to the TCP/IP stack, and then to the Internet software, where the child can view it and interact with it. SurfWatch does all the checking practically instantly, so that there is no apparent delay in getting material from the Internet.

7 Since the Internet is growing so fast, and so many new sites are being created every month, the SurfWatch database of objectionable sites could become outdated. To solve the problem, SurfWatch automatically updates the database of sites every month. That way, the list of sites is always kept current.

Network Server

8 Parents aren't the only people who want to filter out objectionable sites. Many businesses also may want to ensure that their workers aren't accessing objectionable sites over their corporate network. Instead of having a copy of SurfWatch installed on every user's computer, the software is installed on a network server where all Internet traffic must travel through. At the server, the SurfWatch software checks for objectionable sites in the same way it does at individual machines, except when it is on a server, it filters all Internet traffic for the entire company.

INDEX